READY TO WRITE

PERFECTING PARAGRAPHS

FOURTH EDITION

KAREN BLANCHARD • CHRISTINE ROOT

PEARSON
Longman

Ready to Write 2: Perfecting Paragraphs
Fourth Edition

This book was previously published as *Ready to Write, A First Composition Text, Third Edition*.

Pearson Education, 10 Bank Street, White Plains, NY 10606

Acknowledgements: We are grateful to several people whose contributions strengthened this book. Thank you to Lynn Whitnall, Andrea J. Brooks, Daniel L. Blanchard, and Robby Steinberg. Thank you also to our wonderful editorial and production staff: Christopher Leonowicz, Stacey Hunter, and Carlos Rountree. Finally, thanks to Pietro Alongi and Paula Van Ells at Pearson Longman for their steadfast support.
Staff credits: The people who made up the *Ready to Write* team, representing editorial, production, design, and manufacturing, are Pietro Alongi, Gina DiLillo, Nancy Flaggman, Christopher Leonowicz, Amy McCormick, Edith Pullman, Carlos Rountree, Massimo Rubini, Barbara Sabella, Donna Schaffer, Jennifer Stem, Jane Townsend, and Paula Van Ells.
Text composition: TSI Graphics
Text font: 10.5 Frutiger Light
Illustrations: Gary Torrisi
Technical art: Tinge Design Studio, except pp. 86, 88-89, 148, 161, 181, 182 by Lisa Ghiozzi and Paula Williams
Photo credits: Cover and interior by Shutterstock.com unless otherwise noted. Page 36, istockphoto.com; 126, Photo courtesy of David Root; 150, (t) Library of Congress, Prints and Photographs Division (b) Library of Congress, Prints and Photographs Division, Detroit Publishing Company Collection; 163, 192, Photos courtesy of David Root; 197, © Associated Press/Wilfredo Lee
Text credits: Page 88, Reprinted with permission from Open Doors: 2001, The Institute of International Education; 89, Adapted from *The Complete Book of Running*, by James F. Fixx, © 1977 by Simon & Schuster, Inc. PEANUTS reprinted by permission of United Feature Syndicate, Inc.

Library of Congress Cataloging-in-Publication Data
Blanchard, Karen Lourie
 [Ready to write]
 Ready to write 2 : perfecting paragraphs / Karen Blanchard, Christine Root. — 4th ed.
    p. cm.
 Previously published as: Ready to Write, A First Composition Text, 3rd ed., 2002.
 ISBN-13: 978-0-13-136332-8 (pbk.)
 ISBN-10: 0-13-136332-8 (pbk.)
 1. English language—Textbooks for foreign speakers. 2. English language—Composition and exercises. 3. English language—Paragraphs. 4. Report writing—Problems, exercises, etc. I. Root, Christine Baker II. Getting Organized: The key to good writing — Understanding paragraphs — Organizing information by time order — Organizing information by order of importance — Organizing information by spatial order — Understanding the writing process — Supporting the main idea — Explaining a process — Writing descriptions — Expressing your opinion — Comparing and contrasting — Analyzing causes and effects — Writing personal letters and business letters — Writing. III. Title. IV. Title: Ready to write two.
 PE1128.B587 2010
 808'.042—dc22

                      2009030433

ISBN-13: 978-0-13-136332-8
ISBN-10: 0-13-136332-8

4WEST000474261

Printed in the United States of America
4 5 6 7 8 9 10-V011-13 12 11

This book is dedicated to the memory of Karen's father, Dr. Herbert Lourie, whose love of learning was an inspiration to all who knew him; and to the memory of Christine's mother, Charlotte S. Baker, who understood so well the power and magic of the written word.

CONTENTS

SCOPE AND SEQUENCE

CHAPTER	GRAMMAR GUIDE	PARAGRAPH POINTERS/WRITING SKILLS AND STRATEGIES	SAMPLE WRITING TOPICS/ACTIVITIES
1 **GETTING ORGANIZED:** The Key to Good Writing	• Capitalization and Punctuation	• Recognizing ways to organize information into groups • Identifying irrelevant information	• Writing lists (things to do this weekend, places to visit, purchases made in the last month) • Dividing words into groups and writing a topic heading appropriate for each
2 **UNDERSTANDING PARAGRAPHS**	• Compound Sentences	• Identifying parts of a paragraph • Understanding paragraph form • Identifying and developing topic, supporting, and concluding sentences • Turning topic sentences into questions • Understanding paragraph unity	• Using topic sentences as prompts to write paragraphs about the difficulties of learning a new language, the qualities of good teachers, ways to save money on a vacation, and great places to visit • Following steps to write a paragraph about your proudest or most embarrassing moment, best or worst job, etc.
3 **ORGANIZING INFORMATION BY TIME ORDER**	• Prepositions of Time • Complex Sentences with *Before* and *After*	• Recognizing that well-organized paragraphs include transitions, called signal words, to connect ideas • Recognizing and using time-order signal words • Recognizing chronological order	• Using a schedule, to-do lists, and timelines to write paragraphs with signal words to show chronological order • Using prepositions of time to write an e-mail • Researching, planning, and writing a biographical paragraph • Writing a paragraph about a memorable day
4 **ORGANIZING INFORMATION BY ORDER OF IMPORTANCE**	• *Would Rather*	• Ordering supporting information by importance • Recognizing and using signal words for order of importance (*first, in addition, most importantly*)	• Ordering supporting points by importance to write paragraphs about the qualities of a good teacher, choosing a university, etc. • Planning and writing a paragraph about preferences • Writing equal-order paragraphs • Writing an e-mail using signal words

CHAPTER	GRAMMAR GUIDE	PARAGRAPH POINTERS/WRITING SKILLS AND STRATEGIES	SAMPLE WRITING TOPICS/ACTIVITIES
5 **ORGANIZING INFORMATION BY SPATIAL ORDER**	• Prepositions of Place	• Using spatial order to organize details in a descriptive paragraph (start on the left side and move right, go from right to left, start with the outside and move in, etc.)	• Using details to write paragraphs describing floors of buildings • Using a map to write a paragraph describing regions of the U.S. • Writing descriptive paragraphs about a room, stage set, doctor's office, garden, etc.
6 **UNDERSTANDING THE WRITING PROCESS**	• Sentence Fragments	• Recognizing and using the steps of the writing process • Practicing prewriting (brainstorming, clustering, listing) • Organizing ideas into simple, informal outlines • Practicing what to include in a first draft • Using a revising checklist • Editing paragraphs	• Using the writing process to prewrite, write, and revise paragraphs about tips for making new friends, describing a classmate, jobs, sports, movies, vacations, health, and music
7 **SUPPORTING THE MAIN IDEA**	• *For Example*, *For Instance*, *Such As* • Punctuating Quotes	• Choosing appropriate support for main ideas • Using verbs that describe changes to write about charts and graphs • Recognizing and choosing the type of support that best proves the main point (personal anecdotes, reasons, examples, quotations, facts and statistics)	• Using the writing process to write paragraphs with supporting examples; personal anecdotes; facts, statistics, and information from graphs and charts • Writing a paragraph explaining information in a chart or graph • Using unusual facts from the library or Internet to write a paragraph about an animal
8 **EXPLAINING A PROCESS**	• Imperative Sentences	• Recognizing what to include in a topic sentence for a process paragraph • Recognizing how to use time-order signal words to describe steps in a process • Recognizing and using signal words useful for giving directions (*across the street from*, *next door to*, *on the corner*)	• Using the writing process to write paragraphs about how to plan a party, study for an exam, change a flat tire, etc. • Using the writing process to write a lab report about the life cycle of a butterfly • Writing directions • Writing a "how to" paragraph about getting to a place in your hometown, protecting yourself in a natural disaster, etc.

CHAPTER	GRAMMAR GUIDE	PARAGRAPH POINTERS/WRITING SKILLS AND STRATEGIES	SAMPLE WRITING TOPICS/ACTIVITIES
9 **WRITING DESCRIPTIONS**	• Order of Adjectives (opinion, size, age, shape, color, origin, material, purpose)	• Recognizing that a descriptive paragraph about an object should create a picture with words • Recognizing what to include in a topic sentence for a descriptive paragraph • Recognizing and using descriptive details to describe people • Recognizing and using common sensory words to describe objects • Using spatial order and descriptive language	• Using the writing process to write a paragraph describing a person you know • Writing a description of a famous person • Writing descriptions of products on the Internet • Using the writing process to describe something you have lost and something you want to sell • Using the writing process to write paragraphs that describe special places • Describing someone or something in a photo
10 **EXPRESSING YOUR OPINION**	• Run-on Sentences	• Using convincing reasons in a logical order to develop an opinion paragraph • Recognizing what to include in a topic sentence for an opinion paragraph • Recognizing and using phrases useful for beginning a topic sentence in an opinion paragraph • Recognizing and using words that signal order of importance to organize supporting reasons in an opinion paragraph	• Using the writing process to write an opinion paragraph about TV and children, working mothers, nuclear energy, lab experiments on animals, the death penalty, cell phones and driving, etc. • Using the writing process to write opinion paragraphs about drinking and driving; suspects of a computer crime • Responding to letters of advice • Writing an opinion paragraph about marrying someone of a different religion, following a vegetarian diet, etc.
11 **COMPARING AND CONTRASTING**	• Sentence Patterns of Comparison • Comparative Adjectives	• Recognizing and using signal words of comparison • Recognizing and using signal words of contrast • Recognizing what to include in topic sentences for paragraphs that compare and contrast • Recognizing appropriate topics to compare and contrast	• Using the writing process to write paragraphs comparing two people or things • Using the writing process to write a paragraph contrasting two apartments, vacations, job candidates, cultures, etc. • Writing a paragraph comparing two important people, sports teams, types of music, etc.

CHAPTER	GRAMMAR GUIDE	PARAGRAPH POINTERS/WRITING SKILLS AND STRATEGIES	SAMPLE WRITING TOPICS/ACTIVITIES
12 **ANALYZING CAUSES AND EFFECTS**		• Recognizing and using signal words that introduce causes and effects • Recognizing what to include in topic sentences for cause and effect paragraphs • Analyzing situations • Recognizing elements of paragraph unity	• Using the writing process to write paragraphs about the causes of population increase, reasons for an important life decision, and the causes of a business failure • Using the writing process to write a paragraph about the effects of global warming, too much caffeine, important life decisions, etc. • Writing a cause-effect paragraph about immigrating to a new country, an unhealthy habit, or a recent economic or political situation
13 **WRITING PERSONAL LETTERS AND BUSINESS LETTERS**		• Recognizing and using the parts and punctuation of personal and business letters • Recognizing the format for addressing envelopes • Recognizing formal and informal language	• Writing a personal letter to a friend about what's new in your life; inviting a friend to visit you; thanking a relative for a gift; telling your parents about an important decision you've made • Using the writing process to write business letters of request, complaint, and/or praise • Writing business and personal letters of complaint
14 **WRITING SUMMARIES**		• Distinguishing between main ideas and details • Synthesizing information • Recognizing strategies for writing answers to essay questions on exams	• Using the writing process to write one-paragraph summaries of a textbook section, newspaper article, and story • Completing a one-paragraph summary of a folktale • Writing answers to test questions

INTRODUCTION

Ready to Write 2 came about because of our threefold conviction that

- high-beginning and low-intermediate students learn to write well and achieve a more complete English proficiency by learning and practicing writing skills simultaneously with other English language skills they are learning;
- students are interested in and capable of writing expressively in English—however simple the language—on a variety of provocative and sophisticated topics if they are supplied with the basic vocabulary and organizational tools;
- students need to be explicitly taught that different languages organize information differently, and they need to be shown how to organize information correctly in English.

Approach

Based on these assumptions, *Ready to Write 2* is intended to get students writing early in their second language acquisition experience. By providing them with a wide variety of stimulating writing topics and exercises that go beyond sentence manipulation drills, students are encouraged to bring their own ideas and talent to the writing process. With a focus on the process of writing paragraphs, students learn, step by step, the organizational principles that will help them express themselves effectively in English. They also learn to apply these principles to a variety of rhetorical formats.

As in *Ready to Write 1* and *Ready to Write 3*, the activities are designed to encourage students to think independently and to provide them with many opportunities for sharing ideas with their classmates, thus creating a more dynamic learning environment. To this end, collaborative writing and peer feedback activities are included in all the chapters. In addition, great care has been taken to maintain an appropriate level of vocabulary and complexity of sentence structure for high-beginning and low-intermediate students so that the explanations, directions, and readings are easily accessible.

The Fourth Edition

The fourth edition of *Ready to Write 2* includes these important features:

- attention to the writing process with guided practice at each stage, including specific techniques for prewriting, writing, and revising
- numerous and varied paragraph-writing opportunities
- introduction to different patterns of organization, including model paragraphs
- emphasis on parts of a paragraph, with guidance on writing topic sentences, supporting sentences, and concluding sentences
- more specific grammar practice
- activities that emphasize paragraph unity and coherence
- opportunities for students to think creatively

Two popular features from the previous editions—*You Be the Editor* and *On Your Own*—continue to appear regularly in this edition. *You Be the Editor* provides practice in error correction and proofreading in order to help students monitor their own errors. (An Answer Key for this section appears at the end of the book.) *On Your Own* provides students with further individual practice in the paragraph-writing skills they have learned. We hope that you enjoy working through these activities with your students. At any level, they are definitely ready to write. —*KLB and CBR*

GETTING ORGANIZED:
The Key to Good Writing

Writing can be difficult in your own language. In a new language, writing can be even more difficult. The good news is that writing involves skills that you can learn, practice, and master. As you work through this book, you will learn and practice the skills you need to become a good writer in English.

Organization is the key to good writing. Different languages organize ideas differently. In this chapter, you will begin to learn how to organize information in English so that you can write effective paragraphs.

Copyright 2004 by Randy Glasbergen.
www.glasbergen.com

**"I am not disorganized — I know *exactly* where everything is!
The newer stuff is on top and the older stuff is on the bottom."**

ORGANIZING INFORMATION INTO GROUPS

One way to organize information is to group similar ideas together.

Look at the following list of places.

- South America
- New York City
- Italy
- Korea
- Istanbul
- Asia
- Tokyo
- Mexico
- Europe

You can organize this list by dividing it into three groups. Notice that each group has something in common.

A	B	C
South America	Italy	New York City
Asia	Korea	Istanbul
Europe	Mexico	Tokyo

1. What do all the places in group A have in common?

   They are continents.
   _____

2. What do all the places in group B have in common?

   _____

3. What do all the places in group C have in common?

   _____

You can give each group a name. The name is the topic of the list.

A Continents	B Countries	C Cities
South America	Italy	New York City
Asia	Korea	Istanbul
Europe	Mexico	Tokyo

Organizing Lists

Activity 1

Divide the words in each list into three groups. Put similar ideas together and write a topic for each group.

1. Sunday   winter
   January   spring
   ·February   Friday
   summer   December
   Tuesday

A	B	C
Topic: ____days____	Topic: _____	Topic: _____
____Sunday____	_____	_____
____Tuesday____	_____	_____
____Friday____	_____	_____

2.

jet	truck
bus	helicopter
boat	submarine
car	ship
airplane	

A	**B**	**C**
Topic: _____	Topic: _____	Topic: _____
_____	_____	_____
_____	_____	_____
_____	_____	_____

3.

ring	glasses
hat	mittens
shoes	boots
socks	headband
gloves	

A	**B**	**C**
Topic: _____	Topic: _____	Topic: _____
_____	_____	_____
_____	_____	_____
_____	_____	_____

4.

red	medium
small	purple
triangle	circle
square	green
large	

A	**B**	**C**
Topic: _____	Topic: _____	Topic: _____
_____	_____	_____
_____	_____	_____
_____	_____	_____

Activity 2

One word in each list is more general than the others. This word is the topic of the list. Circle the topic.

1. chair
   table
   desk
   (furniture)
   sofa

2. necklace
   ring
   jewelry
   earrings
   watch

3. mail
   postcard
   letter
   bill
   package

4. suitcase
   duffle bag
   luggage
   garment bag
   cosmetics case

5. waterfall
   mountain
   lake
   valley
   scenery

Activity 3

Write a topic for each list on the line. Use your dictionaries if necessary.

1. _____cars_____
   convertibles
   sedans
   station wagons
   sports cars

2. _____
   engineer
   teacher
   lawyer
   dentist

3. _____
   Earth
   Jupiter
   Mars
   Venus

4. _____
   Atlantic
   Pacific
   Indian
   Arctic

5. _____
   earthquake
   flood
   tornado
   avalanche

6. _____
   gold
   silver
   iron
   copper

7. _____
   pediatrician
   surgeon
   cardiologist
   internist

8. _____
   make the beds
   dust the furniture
   vacuum the carpets
   clean the bathroom

Choosing a Way to Organize

Often there is more than one way to organize things into groups. For example, cars can be grouped in several ways.

Topic: cars	**Topic:** cars	**Topic:** cars
full-size	cars that cost less than $15,000	new cars
mid-size	cars that cost between $15,000 and $25,000	used cars
compact	cars that cost more than $25,000	
subcompact		

Activity 1

Work with a partner and complete the following tasks.

1. Think of at least two ways to organize different kinds of sports. Then list the sports for each category.

   Topic: kinds of sports   **Topic:** kinds of sports

   _____   _____

   _____   _____

   _____   _____

   _____   _____

2. Think of at least two ways to organize types of food. Then list the foods for each category.

   Topic: kinds of food   **Topic:** kinds of food

   _____   _____

   _____   _____

   _____   _____

   _____   _____

Activity 2

Make a list of all the people in your class. Organize the list by dividing the people into groups. Think of several ways to do this and write them below. Remember that all members of a group should have something in common.

1. _Divide the students into two groups: males and females_ _____

2. _____

3. _____

4. _____

5. _____

IDENTIFYING IRRELEVANT INFORMATION

All of the items in a group should have something in common. They should also relate to the topic of the group. When an item does not relate to the other items in a group, it does not belong in that group. An item that does not belong is called *irrelevant*.

Activity 1

Cross out the item in each group that does not belong.

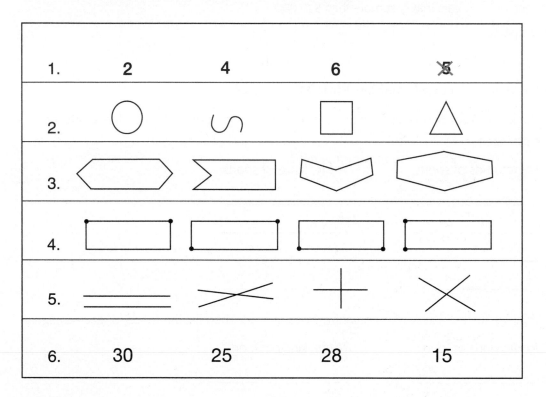

Activity 2

Cross out the word in each group that does not belong. Then write a topic for each list.

1. _eating utensils_
   fork
   ~~oven~~
   spoon
   chopsticks

2. _____
   Pennsylvania
   Denver
   Florida
   California

3. _____
   noun
   comma
   verb
   adjective

4. _____
   Spanish
   Turkish
   Chinese
   Modern

5. _____
   physics
   swimming
   biology
   chemistry

6. _____
   saxophone
   piano
   engine
   drums

7. _____
   computer
   telephone
   fax machine
   washing machine

8. _____
   happy
   windy
   sad
   angry

Activity 3

Cross out the sentence in each group that does not belong.

1. **Topic:** It is interesting to visit foreign countries.
   a. You can meet new people.
   b. You can eat different kinds of food.
   c. ~~It is expensive. You can spend too much money.~~
   d. You can see the way other people live.
   e. You can learn about other cultures.

2. **Topic:** Seattle is a great place to live if you like the outdoors.
   a. The weather is usually warm and pleasant.
   b. The roads are crowded and there is always a lot of traffic.
   c. You can ride a bicycle, go running, or take a walk almost any day of the year.
   d. You can go rock climbing or hiking in the nearby Cascade and Olympic Mountains.
   e. The Pacific Ocean is very close, so it is easy to go fishing, surfing, and swimming.

3. **Topic:** Small cars are becoming more popular.
   a. They are more economical.
   b. Small cars use less gas than bigger cars.
   c. They are easier to park.
   d. Some small cars are uncomfortable.
   e. Small cars are better for the environment.

4. **Topic:** Different people spend their free time in different ways.
   a. Some people spend their free time reading or watching TV.
   b. The price of movies has increased recently.
   c. Other people like to go shopping if they have some free time.
   d. Many people enjoy playing sports or watching their favorite team play.
   e. Some people like to visit their friends in their free time.

5. **Topic:** Nursing is an excellent career choice for some people.
   a. It offers a rewarding opportunity to help other people.
   b. Nurses can find interesting jobs in all areas of health care.
   c. Nurses earn a good salary and have great benefits.
   d. Some universities do not have nursing programs.
   e. Nurses often have flexible work schedules.

6. **Topic:** The new Lewis Convention Center is a great addition to our city.

    a. It creates new jobs.

    b. It brings tourists to our city.

    c. The convention center schedules interesting exhibits.

    d. The building is architecturally pleasing.

    e. There isn't enough parking at the convention center.

GRAMMAR GUIDE: CAPITALIZATION AND PUNCTUATION

Like most other languages, English has certain rules for capitalization and punctuation. Learning these rules will improve your writing.

A. **Review the rules for capitalization and punctuation and read the example sentences.**

RULES	EXAMPLES
1. Begin the first word of every sentence with a capital letter and end it with a period, exclamation point, or question mark.	People around the world drink tea. Look at that beautiful car! Who won the race?
2. Always capitalize the pronoun *I*.	Christine and I wrote this book.
3. Capitalize all proper nouns including • names and titles • names of places (cities, streets, countries, etc.) • names of languages, religions, and nationalities	Dr. Carol Wolf I live at 515 Prospect Avenue in Toronto, Canada. Japanese
4. Capitalize days of the week, holidays, and months of the year, but do not capitalize the names of seasons.	My favorite holiday, Halloween, is next Tuesday. I plant flowers every spring and summer.
5. Capitalize the first word of a quote.	The teacher said, "Please open your books."

B. **Add capital letters and punctuation to the sentences.**

1. engineering is a good career choice for some people

2. my sister and I love japanese food

3. who is your favorite movie star

4. the meeting is scheduled for monday, april 25

5. i made an appointment with dr. brody for friday morning

6. do you know anyone who speaks korean

7. matt and I will meet you on the corner of locust street and second avenue

8. mr. jones said, "the train to burlington, vermont, is running thirty minutes late"

YOU BE THE EDITOR

Read the story. It contains ten errors in capitalization and punctuation. Correct the mistakes. Copy the corrected paragraph on a separate piece of paper.

Many of the stories in my country, turkey, are about a clever man named nasreddin. In one story, nasreddin is walking through the marketplace when an angry shopkeeper stops him The shopkeeper yells at nasreddin for not paying the seventy-five piasters he owes him. But the clever Nasreddin says, "you know that i plan to pay you thirty-five piasters tomorrow, and next tuesday another thirty-five. that means i owe you only five piasters. You should be ashamed for yelling at me so loudly for a debt of only five piasters!" I laugh every time I think of that story.

ON YOUR OWN

Complete the following activity.

1. Choose one of the following topics and make a list.
   * things you have to do this weekend
   * places you want to visit
   * purchases you have made in the last month
2. Organize the items on your list into groups.
3. Give each group a name.

CHAPTER 2
UNDERSTANDING PARAGRAPHS

Most English writing is organized into paragraphs. A paragraph is a group of related sentences. Like the items on each list in Chapter 1, the sentences in a paragraph should all have something in common. They should all relate to the topic.

IDENTIFYING PARTS OF PARAGRAPHS

Most paragraphs follow a certain format. They have three basic parts. A good paragraph begins with a sentence that states the main idea of the whole paragraph. This sentence is called the topic sentence. The next group of sentences in the paragraph explains the main idea. They add details and give support. These sentences are called supporting sentences. Some paragraphs end with a concluding sentence. This sentence restates the main idea.

A. **Read the paragraph. Notice the three basic parts.**

My Class

TOPIC SENTENCE → The students in my class come from many different parts of the world.

SUPPORTING SENTENCES → Some students are from European countries such as Germany and Italy, and others are from Middle Eastern countries such as Saudi Arabia and Israel. Several students were born in Latin American countries, including Peru and Brazil. Most students are from Asian countries such as Korea, China, and Japan.

CONCLUDING SENTENCE → My classmates are an interesting mix of people from many different countries, and we all get along very well.

PARAGRAPH POINTER: Paragraph Form

Remember: A paragraph must be written in a proper form. Follow these rules.
- Indent the first word of each paragraph.
- Leave margins (space on both sides of the paragraph).
- Begin each sentence with a capital letter.
- End each sentence with a period, question mark, or exclamation point.
- Do not start each new sentence on a new line.

B. **Read the following paragraphs and answer the questions.**

1.   There are many reasons why people move. Some move to find better jobs or to advance their careers. Others are attracted to places with better weather. Still others want to move to a place with less crime. Finally, people often want to move to a place with a lower cost of living. For these reasons, every year millions of people move to new places.

a. What is the topic sentence? _____

_____

b. How many supporting sentences are there in the paragraph? _____

c. What is the concluding sentence? _____

_____

2.   More men are now doing jobs that traditionally belonged to women. For example, there are now twice as many male nurses as there were ten years ago. The number of stay-at-home fathers in the United States has increased from 98,000 in 2003 to more than 160,000 today. Similarly, there are many more male secretaries, elementary school teachers, librarians, and bank tellers than ever before. It is clear that ideas about traditionally female occupations have changed.

a. What is the topic sentence? _____

_____

b. How many supporting sentences are there in the paragraph? _____

c. What is the concluding sentence? _____

_____

3.   For thousands of years, garlic has had many uses. The Romans gave garlic to their slaves for strength and to their soldiers for courage. During the Middle Ages, some people used garlic to keep witches away. In the eighteenth century, garlic was used to cure diseases. Even today, some people believe that eating garlic can prevent colds. Garlic has a long history as a plant with many uses.

a. What is the topic sentence? _____

_____

b. How many supporting sentences are there in the paragraph? _____

c. What is the concluding sentence? _____

_____

4.   Today cell phones can do a lot more than just make and receive calls. A lot of cell phones come with cameras that take color pictures. Some cell phones even have video cameras to record live-action events. You can also use a cell phone to check your e-mail on the Internet or set reminders for important events with a special alarm clock. Many cell phones have calculators for solving simple math problems and fun games to play if you're bored. With all of these new features, it is hard to imagine what cell phones of the future will be able to do.

    a.   What is the topic sentence? _____

    _____

    b.   How many supporting sentences are there in the paragraph? _____

    c.   What is the concluding sentence? _____

    _____

5.   The popular game of chess has a long and interesting history. No one knows for sure when chess was invented, but people were playing chess in China and India about 1,400 years ago. From Asia, chess spread to North Africa and then to Europe. The modern form of chess, which we play today, developed in the 1500s in Europe. Today people around the world still play chess with each other or even on their computers. With its long history, chess will probably remain a popular game in the future.

    a.   What is the topic sentence? _____

    _____

    b.   How many supporting sentences are there in the paragraph? _____

    c.   What is the concluding sentence? _____

    _____

TOPIC SENTENCES

The topic sentence is the most important sentence of a paragraph. It states the main idea and introduces the reader to the topic. The topic sentence is more general than the other sentences in the paragraph. Remember that a topic sentence, like all English sentences, must have a subject and a verb.

A topic sentence should have two parts: the **topic** and the **controlling idea**. The topic states the subject of the paragraph. It is what the paragraph is about. The controlling idea limits your topic. It tells what you are going to say about the subject.

Read the following three topic sentences. Each one has the same topic—cell phones— but a different controlling idea.

       ┌─ TOPIC ─┐ ┌────── CONTROLLING IDEA ──────┐
a.   Cell phones make communication much easier.

       ┌─ TOPIC ─┐ ┌──── CONTROLLING IDEA ────┐
b.   Cell phones are an annoying invention.

       ┌─ TOPIC ─┐ ┌──── CONTROLLING IDEA ────┐
c.   Cell phones keep improving every year.

Activity 1

Draw a circle around the topic and underline the controlling idea in each sentence.

1. Written exams make me nervous.

2. Colors have different meanings around the world.

3. Miles Davis is my favorite jazz musician.

4. There are several advantages to growing up in a small town.

5. The computer was the greatest invention of the twentieth century.

6. The Cannes Film Festival is the largest and most famous film festival in the world.

Activity 2

Complete each topic sentence by adding a controlling idea.

1. Good drivers _____

2. Public transportation _____

3. Television _____

4. My parents _____

5. My first day of school _____

Identifying Topic Sentences

Choose the best topic sentence for each paragraph. Write it on the line provided.

1. _Skiing is my favorite sport._ I usually go skiing every weekend in the winter even though it is expensive. I love the feeling of flying down a mountain. The views are beautiful from the top of a mountain and along the trails. Even the danger of falling and getting hurt can't keep me away from the slopes on a winter day.
   a. Skiing is expensive.
   b. Skiing is my favorite sport.
   c. Skiing is dangerous.

2. _____ North Americans send cards for many occasions. They send cards to family and friends on birthdays and holidays. They also send thank-you cards, get-well cards, graduation cards, and congratulation cards. It is very common to buy cards in stores and send them through the mail, but sending e-cards over the Internet is also popular.
   a. Sending cards is very popular in North America.
   b. Birthday cards are the most popular kind of card.
   c. It is important to send thank-you cards.

3. _____ I enjoy summer sports like water skiing and baseball. The weather is usually sunny and hot, so I can go to the beach almost every day. Gardening is my hobby, and I spend many summer days working in my garden. Unfortunately, the days pass too quickly in summer.
   a. I like to garden in the summer.
   b. Summer is my favorite season.
   c. Summer is too short.

4. _____ First of all, our coach is always late for practice so the team never has enough time to train. Also, he is very mean during the games and yells at the players rather than giving them advice on how to improve. Finally, we need a new coach because our current coach doesn't even know how to play soccer well!
   a. My soccer team has a horrible coach.
   b. A good soccer coach should be able to play soccer well.
   c. Soccer is my favorite sport.

5. _____ For example, a person can have breakfast in New York and fly to Paris for dinner. A businesswoman in London can place an order with a factory in Hong Kong instantly by sending a fax. People can use a webcam to have a meeting without leaving their offices.
   a. Airplanes have changed our lives.
   b. Advances in technology have made the world seem smaller.
   c. The fax machine was an important invention.

6. _____ One thing you must consider is the quality of the university's educational program. You also need to think about the school's size and location. Finally, you must be sure to consider the university's tuition to make sure you can afford to go to school there.
   a. It is expensive to attend a university in the United States.
   b. There are several factors to consider when you choose a university to attend.
   c. You should consider getting a good education.

7. _____ One type of reality television show is the competition-based program. In these shows, contestants go through a series of challenges, and whoever wins the most challenges at the end of the season gets a big prize. Another type of popular reality show is the documentary-based type. In these shows, viewers watch people going about their daily lives and facing everyday challenges. Finally, there are instructional reality shows. For example, there are shows that can teach you how to cook a delicious meal in thirty minutes or redecorate your living room without spending too much money.
   a. There are many types of reality shows on television today.
   b. Reality shows are my favorite type of television programs.
   c. Anyone can learn to cook just by watching television.

Writing Topic Sentences

Write a topic sentence for each of the following paragraphs. Make sure your topic sentence includes a topic and a controlling idea. Then share your topic sentences with your classmates by writing them on the board. Discuss the differences.

> **PARAGRAPH POINTER:** Topic Sentence
>
> Turn your topic sentence into a question. The rest of the paragraph should answer this question. If the rest of your paragraph doesn't answer this question, then your topic sentence probably doesn't fit the content of the paragraph, or the other sentences don't support the topic sentence.

1. _Miami is the perfect place to take a vacation._ It is always sunny and warm. The beaches are gorgeous, with soft white sand and beautiful water. There are many fine restaurants in the Miami area, and most of the hotels offer terrific nightly entertainment. It's no wonder that Miami is my first choice for a vacation destination.

2. _____ He has collected stamps and coins ever since he was a child. He is very proud of his valuable collections. Paul also enjoys painting and drawing. Recently he has become interested in gardening. Out of all of his hobbies, Paul's favorite one is reading. He usually reads at least one book every week. Paul keeps busy with all of his hobbies.

3. _____ I can't wait to come home from school and eat the delicious meals she has prepared. My mother is famous for her desserts, like peach pie and chocolate soufflé. She is always experimenting with new recipes and trying different ingredients. No one in the world can cook the way my mother does.

4. _____ First, and most importantly, the work is very interesting. I learn new things every day and I get to travel a lot. In addition, my boss is very nice. She is always willing to help me when I have a problem. I have also made many new friends at my job. Last but not least, the salary is fantastic. I plan on staying at this job for a long time.

5. _____ For one thing, feathers help birds by keeping them warm and dry. Colorful feathers also play an important part in attracting mates. The colors of a bird's feathers can also provide camouflage and protect it from predators. Finally, the main purpose of feathers is to help birds fly.

6. _____ The small size and light weight are both appealing features. iPods are easy to carry in your pocket, handbag, or backpack. They may be small, but iPods can store and play thousands of songs. Another advantage is that iPods can organize your music. The songs you store on an iPod are automatically grouped by musical type, such as rock, popular, jazz, or classical. They are also listed by performer. You can use your iPod to listen to audiobooks and lectures. You can see why I never go out without my iPod.

SUPPORTING SENTENCES

The supporting sentences develop the main idea stated in the topic sentence. The supporting details are more specific than the main idea. Their purpose is to help readers understand more about your main idea. Supporting sentences can give examples, facts, explanations, or reasons. Supporting sentences often tell *who, what, when, where, why, how, how much,* or *how many.*

Identifying Supporting Sentences

Read the following paragraphs and underline the supporting sentences.

1. Use of the Internet has grown very quickly. In 1983, there were 562 computers connected to the Internet, but by the turn of the century, there were 72.3 million computers in 247 countries online. Experts say that the Internet is now growing at a rate of approximately 50 to 60 percent a year. As time goes on, the Internet is becoming more and more popular.

2. There are many reasons I hate my apartment. First of all, the windows are small and the apartment is never sunny. I also have noisy neighbors who keep me up all night. The air conditioner doesn't work properly, so it's too hot in the summer. Finally, there are so many bugs in my apartment that I could start an insect collection. I really want to move!

3. Vegetables and fruits are an important part of a healthy diet. First, fruits and vegetables are packed with the vitamins and minerals you need to keep your body functioning smoothly. In addition, they give you the carbohydrates you need for energy. Fruits and vegetables have lots of fiber to help your digestive system work properly. Finally, many scientists believe that the nutrients in fruits and vegetables can help fight diseases. If you eat a diet rich in fruits and vegetables, you'll be on the road to better health.

Writing Supporting Sentences

Write three supporting sentences for each topic sentence. Compare your sentences with a partner's.

1. There are several reasons why I am learning English.

   a. _____

   b. _____

   c. _____

2. My hometown is an interesting (or boring) place to visit.

a. _____

b. _____

c. _____

3. I am usually an optimistic (or pessimistic) person.

a. _____

b. _____

c. _____

CONCLUDING SENTENCES

Some paragraphs end with a concluding sentence. This sentence restates the main idea of the paragraph using different words. It summarizes the main points of the paragraph or makes a final comment on the topic. Concluding sentences are not always necessary. In fact, short paragraphs or paragraphs that are part of longer pieces of writing often do not have concluding sentences.

Choosing Concluding Sentences

Choose the best concluding sentence for each paragraph. Write it on the line provided.

1.   Like most Koreans, I love kimchi. Kimchi is the most popular food in Korea. In fact, Koreans serve kimchi as a side dish at almost every meal. Kimchi is made of pickled vegetables and spices, and it's very hot and spicy. Koreans enjoy more than 100 different kinds of kimchi! This delicious food can be eaten alone or mixed with rice or noodles. Luckily, since I eat a lot of it, kimchi is very nutritious. It has vitamins, lactic acid, and minerals. _____

_____

a. If you visit Korea, I hope you will try kimchi.

b. I love all kinds of spicy food.

c. Pho is the most popular food in Vietnam.

2.   My sister Ellen is one of the worst drivers I know. First of all, she is always talking on her cell phone while she drives. To make matters worse, she doesn't pay attention to road signs or speed limits. Sometimes, she puts on lipstick while she's at a red light and doesn't notice when the light turns green. Finally, she often forgets to use her turn signal when she's making a turn. _____

_____

a. I won't be surprised if Ellen gets into an accident soon.

b. Ellen has never gotten a speeding ticket.

c. Ellen's new car is a hybrid; it uses less gas than a regular car.

3.   Breakfast is the most important meal of the day. After sleeping all night, breakfast gives your body the boost of energy it needs to start the day. Eating a healthy breakfast helps you think more clearly and even improves your memory. Studies show that children who eat a nutritious breakfast are more alert and do better in school. Similarly, adults who eat breakfast perform better at work. _____

_____

    a.   Some people skip breakfast and eat a big dinner.
    b.   Children who study hard usually do better in school.
    c.   My mother was right all along when she said, "Remember to eat a good breakfast."

Writing Concluding Sentences

Write a concluding sentence for each paragraph. Then share your concluding sentences with your classmates by writing them on the board. Discuss the differences.

1.   There are many reasons why I like wearing a uniform to school. First of all, it saves time. I don't have to spend time picking out my clothes every morning. Wearing a uniform also saves money. It's cheaper to purchase a few uniforms than to go out and buy lots of school clothes. In addition, I don't have the pressure of keeping up with the latest styles. Most importantly, wearing a school uniform gives me a sense that I belong. I really think it adds to the feeling of school spirit and community.

_____

_____

2.   There are many reasons why I am against wearing my school uniform. For one thing, I don't like the style of the uniform. The navy blazer and plaid skirt are too conservative for me. Secondly, the uniform isn't comfortable. I prefer to wear baggy pants and a sweater instead of a skirt and jacket. Finally, I want the freedom to express my individuality through my style of dressing. _____

_____

3.   Credit cards have a lot of advantages. First of all, credit cards are convenient because you don't have to carry a lot of cash around. You can buy the products and services you need even if you do not have cash in your pocket. In addition, credit cards are very helpful in emergencies. Finally, you can become a better money manager as you learn to use credit cards responsibly. _____

_____

4.   I don't use credit cards anymore for several reasons. First of all, credit cards enable me to spend more money than I have. When I get the bill, I never have enough money in the bank to pay the whole amount. That leads to the second problem—the high interest rate credit card companies charge. Every month I end up paying a lot of money in interest on the amount I still owe on my account. Finally, credit cards are not always the safest way to pay for things. If someone gets your credit card number or steals your card, you may be a victim of credit card fraud. _____

_____

PUTTING IT ALL TOGETHER

Activity 1

A. **Read and discuss the following sentences about Springfield Academy, a boarding school for high school students. Four of the sentences are about the quality of education. Label these Q. Four are about the rules of the school. Label these R. Four sentences relate to the athletic department. Label these A.**

__Q__ 1. Springfield Academy is famous for the high quality of its education.

_____ 2. The athletic director and all the team coaches are excellent.

_____ 3. Students are not allowed to leave campus without permission.

_____ 4. Every year several Springfield graduates receive athletic scholarships to college.

_____ 5. Students are required to wear uniforms.

_____ 6. The library and laboratories have the newest computers and equipment.

_____ 7. Most of its graduates attend very good universities.

_____ 8. It has a new gymnasium, an Olympic-size pool, clay tennis courts, and great playing fields.

_____ 9. Many of the students at Springfield Academy feel that the rules are too strict.

10. Students who do not maintain a B average are put on probation.

_____ 11. The teachers and academic counselors are excellent.

_____ 12. Springfield Academy is known for its wonderful athletic department.

B. **Divide the sentences from Exercise A into three groups. Remember to put similar ideas together. One sentence in each group is general enough to be a topic sentence. Put a check (✔) next to that sentence.**

Quality of Education

✔ Springfield Academy is famous for the high quality of its education.

The library and laboratories have the newest computers and equipment.

_____

_____

Rules of the School

_____

_____

_____

_____

_____

_____

_____

_____

C. Write the sentences from the first group. Begin with the topic sentence. Then write the supporting sentences. Add your own concluding sentence.

_____

_____

_____

_____

_____

_____

D. Write the sentences from the second group. Begin with the topic sentence. Then write the supporting sentences. Add your own concluding sentence.

_____

_____

_____

_____

_____

_____

E. Write the sentences from the third group. Begin with the topic sentence. Then write the supporting sentences. Add your own concluding sentence.

_____

_____

_____

_____

_____

_____

_____

Activity 2

A. **Read the following sentences about San Francisco. Discuss them with your partner. Two of the sentences are topic sentences, and the rest are supporting sentences. Write *TS* in front of each topic sentence and *SS* in front of each supporting sentence.**

_SS_   1. San Francisco is usually warm and pleasant during the day.

_____   2. Some of the country's most famous restaurants and hotels are in San Francisco.

_____   3. There are many things to see and do in San Francisco.

_____   4. There many interesting tourist attractions, such as Fisherman's Wharf and the Golden Gate Bridge.

_____   5. It is never too hot or too cold.

_____   6. The weather in San Francisco is very pleasant.

_____   7. The nightlife is exciting.

_____   8. San Francisco has art galleries, a ballet company, an opera house, and an orchestra.

_____   9. It is cool and breezy at night.

_____ 10. The winters are mild and it rarely snows.

B. **Write the two topic sentences on the lines provided. Then list the supporting sentences under the topic sentences.**

Topic Sentence 1

_____

Supporting Sentences

San Francisco is usually warm and pleasant during the day.
_____
_____
_____

Topic Sentence 2

_____

Supporting Sentences

_____
_____
_____
_____

C. **Write the sentences from the first group in paragraph form. Add your own concluding sentence.**

_____

_____

_____

_____

_____

_____

D. **Now write the sentences from the second group in paragraph form. Add your own concluding sentence.**

_____

_____

_____

_____

_____

_____

_____

PARAGRAPH UNITY

PARAGRAPH POINTER: Unity

Every paragraph must have a single focus. That means that all the supporting sentences in a paragraph must relate to the main idea stated in the topic sentence. A sentence that does not support the main idea is called an _irrelevant sentence_. It does not belong in the paragraph. When all of the sentences support the main idea, the paragraph has unity.

Read this paragraph again. Cross out the sentence that does not belong.

The students in my class come from many different parts of the world. Some students are from European countries such as Germany and Italy, and others are from Middle Eastern countries such as Saudi Arabia and Israel. Several students were born in Latin American countries, including Peru and Brazil. The food in Mexico is delicious. Most students are from Asian countries such as Korea, China, and Japan. My classmates are an interesting mix of people from many different countries, and we all get along very well.

The main idea of the paragraph is that the students in the class come from many different parts of the world. The fact that Mexican food is delicious may be true, but it does not support the main idea.

Activity 1

Read the following sentences. Put a check (✔) next to each sentence that could be added to the preceding paragraph because it supports the main idea.

_____ 1. Several of the students are from African countries.

_____ 2. Half of the students are women.

_____ 3. A few of the students were born in Turkey.

_____ 4. Two students are from Indonesia.

_____ 5. Most of the students are between eighteen and twenty-five years old.

Activity 2

One sentence in each paragraph does not relate to the topic. Find that sentence and cross it out.

1. Cats make wonderful house pets. They are very loving and friendly. Cats are also clean. They don't eat much, so they are not expensive to feed. Unfortunately, some people are allergic to their hair. Cats look beautiful, and they're fun to have in your home.

2. There are several ways people can conserve natural resources. One way is to turn off lights and appliances when they are not in use. Another way is to drive cars less often. My favorite kind of car is a convertible. People can also insulate their houses better. Finally, by reusing things like bottles and plastic bags, people can reduce the amount of waste. By practicing these simple guidelines, we can save our natural resources.

3. The capital city of a country is usually a very important city. The government offices are located in the capital city, and political leaders usually live there or nearby. There are many different types of governments in the world. The capital may also be the center of culture. There are often museums, libraries, and universities in the capital. Finally, the capital city can serve as a center of trade, industry, and commerce, so it is often the financial center of the country.

4. The Japanese automobile industry uses robots in many stages of its production process. In fact, one large Japanese auto factory uses robots in all of its production stages. Some Japanese universities are developing medical robots to detect certain kinds of cancer. Another automobile factory in Japan uses them to paint cars as they come off the assembly line. Furthermore, most Japanese factories use robots to weld the parts of the finished car together.

5.   The packaging of many products is very wasteful. Often the packaging is twice as big as the product. Packaging is used to protect things that are breakable. Many food items, for example, have several layers of unnecessary extra packaging. Most of these extra layers could and should be eliminated, especially since packaging accounts for most of the litter found on streets, in streams, and in parks. I hope companies will start to pay more attention to the way their products are packaged.

GRAMMAR GUIDE: COMPOUND SENTENCES

When you write in English you can combine two simple sentences using coordinating conjunctions such as *and*, *but*, *so*, and *or* to make compound sentences. This will make your writing more interesting.

A. **Study the chart.**

COORDINATING CONJUNCTION	PURPOSE	EXAMPLE
and	joins two similar ideas together	Jane and Catherine went to a movie, **and** they really enjoyed it.
but	joins two contrasting ideas	I wanted to go to the party, **but** I was too sick.
so	connects a reason and a result	Jenny misses her boyfriend, **so** she keeps a picture of him on her desk.
or	joins two alternative ideas	You can call me, **or** you can send me an e-mail.

B. **Look at the paragraph "My Class" on page 10 and underline the compound sentences.**

C. **Work with a partner. Combine each set of sentences into a compound sentence with a coordinating conjunction.**

1. Australia is the smallest continent. It has many types of landscapes.

   Australia is the smallest continent, but it has many types of landscapes.

2. Our computers are old and outdated. We are raising money to buy new ones.

   _____

   _____

3. Children enter the world lacking the skills to take care of themselves. Parents must nurture and protect children when they are young.

_____

_____

4. The family is the basic social unit in every culture. Its structure varies widely among different cultures.

_____

_____

5. Women around the world have won important rights during the last hundred years. Gender inequality still exists in many places.

_____

_____

6. Scientists from all over the world go to Antarctica to study the weather and climate. They go to research the geology and wildlife.

_____

_____

7. In the early days of photography, cameras were big and bulky. Pictures were made on individual glass plates.

_____

_____

8. I have been trying to lose weight for several months. I can't stop eating fattening things like cookies and sodas.

_____

_____

Activity 1

A. **Work with your classmates. Read the following topic sentence.**

It is difficult to learn a new language.

B. **What ideas can you and your classmates think of to support this topic sentence? As you think of ideas, your teacher will write them in list form on the board. Remember, these are just ideas, so they don't have to be complete sentences or in correct order. Copy the list here.**

_____

_____

_____

_____

_____

C. **Discuss the list with your classmates. Cross out details that don't belong.**

D. **With your classmates and teacher, choose the best ideas from your list. Write them in sentence form on the board. Copy the sentences onto the following lines.**

_____

_____

_____

_____

_____

E. **With your classmates and teacher, organize the sentences and put them in correct paragraph form. Your teacher will write the paragraph on the board. Try to include some compound sentences in your paragraph. Copy the finished paragraph here.**

_____

_____

_____

_____

_____

_____

Activity 2

A. **Choose one of the following topic sentences to write about.**
- Good teachers have several important qualities.
- There are several ways to save money when you take a vacation.
- _____ is a great place to visit.

B. Make a list of supporting ideas. You do not have to write the list in complete sentences.

Supporting Ideas

_____

_____

_____

_____

_____

C. Cross out any ideas that do not support the topic sentence.

D. Write the items on your list in complete sentences.

_____

_____

_____

_____

E. Write a paragraph based on your list. Remember to begin with the topic sentence. Include at least one compound sentence. Add a concluding sentence at the end of your paragraph.

_____

_____

_____

_____

_____

_____

_____

F. Form small groups and share your paragraph with the other members of your group.

YOU BE THE EDITOR

Read the paragraph. It contains nine mistakes. Correct the mistakes.
Copy the corrected paragraph on a separate piece of paper.

Erik enjoy many types of sports. He is liking team sports such as basketball, soccer, and baseball. In fact, he is the Captain of the basketball team at our school. erik also plays individual sports like squash, tennis, and golf very good. Last year he win two golf tournaments and most of the tennis matches he played. His favorites sports involve dangerous as well as excitement. He is no afraid to go extreme skiing or skydiving. It was not a surprise when Erik won the sports award at graduation this year.

ON YOUR OWN

Write a paragraph about one of the following topics.
- your proudest or most embarrassing moment
- your best or worst job
- your best friend
- your favorite kind of music, movies, literature, or art

Follow these steps:

1. Write a topic sentence.
2. Make a list of supporting details.
3. Think about the ideas on your list. Cross out any idea that does not support your topic sentence.
4. Write your list in complete sentences.
5. Use the topic and supporting sentences to write a paragraph.
6. Write a concluding sentence.

ORGANIZING INFORMATION BY TIME ORDER

Copyright 2003 by Randy Glasbergen.
www.glasbergen.com

STRESS MANAGEMENT TECHNIQUES
1. _____
2. _____
3. _____
4. _____

"Howl at an ambulance or fire siren every chance you get.
Run around the room in circles with a sock in your mouth.
Eat a messy meal without using your hands or utensils.
Ask a friend to scratch your belly..."

In Chapter 1, you learned that organization is the key to good writing. There are several ways to organize sentences in a paragraph. Three common ways include:

- time order
- order of importance
- spatial order

In this chapter you will practice organizing ideas by time order. When you tell a story, you organize the events in the story as they occurred in time. You tell what happened first at the beginning of the story. Then you tell what happened second, third, and so on. In writing, you often do the same thing.

Read the paragraph and answer the questions.

A Terrible Day

I had a terrible day yesterday. First, I woke up an hour late because my alarm clock didn't go off. From then on, everything went wrong. I burned my hand when I was making breakfast. After I ate breakfast, I got dressed so quickly that I forgot to wear socks. Next, I ran out of the house trying to get the 9:30 bus, but, of course, I missed it. I wanted to take a taxi, but I didn't have enough money. Finally, I walked the 3 miles to my office only to discover that it was Sunday! I hope I never have a day as bad as the one I had yesterday.

1. What is the topic sentence?

_____

2. How are the supporting sentences organized?

   _____

3. What is the concluding sentence?

   _____

SIGNAL WORDS

> **PARAGRAPH POINTER: Signal Words**
>
> A well-organized paragraph often includes signal words (also called transitions) to connect ideas in a paragraph. Signal words help guide the reader from one idea to the next. They are like traffic signals that help you when you are driving. There are many types of signal words.

When you write a paragraph using time order, you should use some of these signal words to explain the order of events.

SIGNAL WORDS THAT SHOW TIME ORDER				
after	finally	last	next	then
before	first	later	second	

Activity 1

Underline the signal words in the paragraph "A Terrible Day" on page 29.

Activity 2

Complete the paragraph with signal words.

> Mornings are my busiest time of day. _____ my alarm goes off at 6 A.M. and I jump out of bed. _____ I rush to the kitchen to make breakfast for my husband and children. _____ I wake everyone else up and get dressed for work. At 7:00 we eat a quick breakfast. I eat very quickly because right _____ breakfast, I have to pack lunches for my kids and make sure they are ready for school. My husband leaves for work at 7:30. Luckily he drops the kids off at school so I have a few minutes to get myself together _____ I go to work. _____, I leave the house at 7:45 and rush to catch the 8 o'clock train to my office. By the time I sit down at my desk, I'm already exhausted.

RECOGNIZING TIME ORDER

Activity 1

A. Look at the pictures. They are all from one comic strip, but they are not in the right order. When you put the pictures in the right order, they tell a funny story. Discuss the pictures with a partner and number them 1 to 4 so they tell the story in the right order. The dog's name is Snoopy.

a. _____   b. _____   c. _____   d. _____

B. Write a sentence about each picture in Exercise A.

1. _____

2. _____

3. _____

4. _____

Activity 2

Read the topic sentence. Then read the sentences that follow it. Together they tell a story. The sentences are not in the correct order. Number them so they follow a logical time order. Then use all of the sentences to write a paragraph.

1. José saved his money and spent two months traveling around the world.

_____ He spent a week in New York and then flew to London and enjoyed several weeks in Europe.

_____ When he had seen the sights in Europe, José took a train to Istanbul and visited many places in Asia.

_1_ First, he flew from his home in Mexico City to New York City.

_____ After he traveled through Asia, he went to South America and finally back home to Mexico.

_____

_____

_____

_____

_____

2. Tim had a hard time keeping his New Year's resolutions.

_____ As the months went on, he broke even more resolutions.

_____ On January 1, he wrote a list of New Year's resolutions.

_____ At the end of January, Tim had broken half of the resolutions.

_____ When the year ended, he realized that he had not kept a single resolution.

_____

_____

_____

_____

3. Mark decided that he wanted to plant a vegetable garden.

_____ At the end of the summer, he picked the vegetables from the garden.

_____ First, he went to a garden store and bought seeds.

_____ Then he went home, prepared the soil, and planted the seeds.

_____ Every day, Mark watered and weeded the garden.

_____

_____

_____

_____

GRAMMAR GUIDE: PREPOSITIONS OF TIME

A. **Study the chart. Circle the prepositions of time in the paragraph on page 29.**

RULES FOR PREPOSITIONS OF TIME	EXAMPLES
Use **at** with specific times.	**at** 5:00 / **at** 7:30 / **at** noon / **at** midnight
Use **from** and **to** with a span of time.	**from** 6:00 *to* 9:00 / **from** 1941 *to* 1945
Use **in** with other parts of the day.	**in** the afternoon / **in** the morning / **in** the evening (exception: **at** night)
Use **in** with months.	**in** August / **in** June
Use **in** with years.	**in** 2009 / **in** 2010
Use **in** with seasons.	**in** the spring / **in** the summer / **in** the winter
Use **on** with days of the week.	**on** Sunday / **on** Tuesday / **on** Friday
Use **on** with specific dates.	**on** June 30 / **on** April 21, 2010 / **on** New Year's Eve

B. Complete the sentences with the correct prepositions.

1. I lived in Detroit _____ 1995 _____ 1998.

2. Lynn was born _____ 1952.

3. She was born _____ October 31, _____ 4:00 _____ the afternoon.

4. I'll meet you for lunch _____ Tuesday _____ noon.

5. Ruth goes to New York every weekend. _____ Saturday she takes the train _____ 9:00 _____ the morning and arrives in New York at 10:45.

C. **You saw this announcement for a Jon McLaughlin concert in the newspaper. Write an e-mail to a friend. Tell your friend about the concert and invite him or her to go with you. Be sure to use correct prepositions of time.**

WORLD CAFÉ LIVE
Presents
Jon McLaughlin

3025 Walnut St.
215-555-1400
$19–$24
Friday 7/11 10 P.M.

| Send | Reply | Forward | Move | Print | Delete | ▲ | ▼ |

Subject: Jon McLaughlin concert

From:

To:

Activity 1

Dr. Alden is the director of an English language school. Study his schedule for Tuesday, February 9. Write a paragraph about his day. Remember to begin with a topic sentence. Use signal words to guide the reader.

My Calendar	February 9 ▲ ▼
8:30–9:00	greet new students
9:00–10:30	give test to new students
10:30–11:30	order textbooks
11:30–12:00	check e-mail
12:00–1:00	have lunch meeting with staff
1:00–3:00	observe classes
3:00–5:00	attend curriculum meeting
5:00–7:00	lead city tour with new students

_____

_____

_____

_____

_____

_____

_____

_____

_____

_____

A. **Vicki is having a birthday dinner for her friend. She made a list of things she has to do before the party. She put the things on her list in time order. Use her list to write a paragraph about the things she has to do. Remember to begin with a topic sentence. Use signal words to guide the reader.**

> TO DO...
> buy food for dinner at supermarket
> pick up birthday cake at bakery
> clean house
> make dinner
> wrap present
> set table

_____

_____

_____

_____

_____

_____

_____

_____

_____

B. **Vicki's dinner party was a success. But she was busy the next day, too. Look at her TO DO list and write a paragraph about her day on a separate piece of paper.**

> TO DO...
> vacuum living room
> empty the dishwasher
> go to the gym
> meet Mom for lunch
> do laundry
> study for Spanish test

Activity 3

Elizabeth Blackwell was the first female medical doctor in the United States. The following time line gives you information about her life. Use the timeline to write a paragraph about her life. Remember to begin with a topic sentence. Use signal words to guide the reader.

February 3, 1821:	born in Bristol, England
1832:	emigrated to New York City
1849:	graduated from Geneva Medical School in Geneva, New York
1853:	opened the New York Infirmary because, as a woman, she could not get a job in a hospital
1868:	opened the Women's Medical College of the New York Infirmary
1875:	assisted in founding the London School of Medicine for Women
1910:	died in Hastings, England

_____

_____

_____

_____

_____

_____

_____

_____

_____

_____

_____

Activity 4

Yao Ming is a famous Chinese basketball player in America and the tallest person playing for the National Basketball Association. The following timeline gives you information about his life. Use the timeline to write a paragraph about his life. Remember to write a topic sentence and include signal words to guide the reader.

September 12, 1980:	born in Shanghai, China, to very tall parents
1989:	entered a junior sports school in China and started to play basketball for the first time
1997:	joined the senior Shark Basketball Team in China and led them to their first championship
2002:	tried out for the NBA and became the first international player to be chosen first by an American team (the Houston Rockets)
2004:	participated in the Summer Olympics and carried the Chinese flag in the opening ceremonies
2005–2008:	broke his foot and knee and had several surgeries in the United States and China
Summer 2008:	played for a Chinese basketball team

_____

_____

_____

_____

_____

_____

_____

_____

_____

_____

_____

_____

GRAMMAR GUIDE: COMPLEX SENTENCES WITH *BEFORE* AND *AFTER*

You have learned that a compound sentence is formed by joining two simple sentences with a coordinating conjunction. Another kind of sentence is called a complex sentence. A complex sentence is formed by joining an independent clause with a dependent clause.

An *independent clause* is a like a simple sentence. It has a subject, a verb, and expresses a complete thought.

A *dependent clause* also has a subject and verb, but it does not express a complete thought. A dependent clause always begins with a subordinating conjunction. There are many words in the English language that function as subordinating conjunctions. In this chapter you will practice using two of them: *before* and *after*.

A. **Read these complex sentences. Notice that the dependent clause can come at the beginning or end of a sentence.**

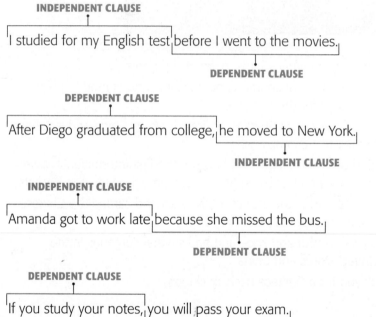

INDEPENDENT CLAUSE

I studied for my English test before I went to the movies.

DEPENDENT CLAUSE

DEPENDENT CLAUSE

After Diego graduated from college, he moved to New York.

INDEPENDENT CLAUSE

INDEPENDENT CLAUSE

Amanda got to work late because she missed the bus.

DEPENDENT CLAUSE

DEPENDENT CLAUSE

If you study your notes, you will pass your exam.

INDEPENDENT CLAUSE

When the dependent clause comes at the beginning of the sentence, use a comma to separate it from the independent clause.

Writers use *before* or *after* to introduce a dependent clause that tells when something happens in relation to the independent clause.

B. **Look at the schedule. Then study the chart.**

| 12:30 | I ate lunch. | 1:00 | I took a nap. | 2:00 | I went to the library. |

EXPLANATION	EXAMPLES
After describes the first action.	**After** I ate lunch, I took a nap. (This means: First, I ate lunch. Then, I took a nap.)
Before describes the second action.	**Before** I went to the library, I took a nap. (This means: First I took a nap. Then I went to the library.)

C. Look at the schedule. Write complex sentences with *before* or *after*, based on the schedule. Put the dependent time clause first.

7:00 A.M. got up	**10:00** A.M. checked in	**12:15** P.M. took a nap
7:15 A.M. ate breakfast	**10:15** A.M. waited at my gate	**2:00** P.M. The plane landed.
7:45 A.M. got dressed	**11:30** A.M. The plane took off.	**2:10** P.M. called my friend to pick me up
9:00 A.M. drove to airport	**11:45** A.M. read a magazine	**2:20** P.M. got off the plane

1. I ate breakfast. I got dressed. (before)

   Before I got dressed, I ate breakfast

2. I drove to the airport. I got dressed. (after)

   After I got

3. I checked in. I waited at my gate. (after)

   _____

4. The plane took off. I read a magazine. (after)

   _____

5. I read a magazine. I took a nap. (after)

   _____

6. I called my friend to pick me up. I got off the plane. (before)

   _____

WRITING PARAGRAPHS WITH TIME ORDER   PART 2

A. Choose a memorable day in your life. Make a list of the important events of the day. Organize your list according to time order.

_____	_____
_____	_____
_____	_____
_____	_____

B. Write a topic sentence for your paragraph. You may fill in the blanks in the following sample or write your own.

_____ was one of the _____ days of my life.

C. Use your list to write a paragraph about the day you chose. Don't forget to begin with a topic sentence and use signal words to guide the reader. Include at least one complex sentence with a dependent time clause.

_____

_____

_____

_____

_____

_____

_____

_____

_____

_____

_____

YOU BE THE EDITOR

Read the paragraph. It contains twelve mistakes. Correct the mistakes. Copy the corrected paragraph on a separate piece of paper.

Throughout history, people have done mathematical computations and kept accounts. in early times, people used groups of sticks or stones to help make calculations. Then the abacus was developed in china. This simple methods represent the beginnings of data processing? As computational needs became more complicated, people developed more advanced technologies. In 1642, Blaise pascal developed the first simple adding machine in france. Later, in England in 1830, charles Babbage designed the first machine that did calculations and printing out results. Finally, In the middle of the twentieth century, researchers at the University of pennsylvania builded the first electronic computer. Today, of course, we have the computer to perform all kinds of advanced .mathematical computations.

ON YOUR OWN

Choose a famous person who interests you. Find information about his or her life. Make a timeline based on the information and write a paragraph.

CHAPTER 4

ORGANIZING INFORMATION BY ORDER OF IMPORTANCE

A clear pattern of organization helps your reader understand your ideas. In Chapter 3, you learned how to organize the information in a paragraph according to time order.

Another common way to organize information is by order of importance. When you use this pattern, you list your ideas from most important to least important or least important to most important.

Read the paragraph and underline the topic sentence. Then answer the questions.

A Great Experience

Volunteering for an organization called Habitat for Humanity was one of the best experiences of my life. First of all, spending the summer helping to build a house taught me a lot of new skills that will come in handy because I plan to get a job in construction. Secondly, I met many new people working on the project. Some of them became good friends. Most importantly, I found deep personal satisfaction helping others. Volunteering really helped me as much as it helped the people who are moving into the house I helped build. I'll never forget my experience at Habitat for Humanity.

1. What three reasons does the author give to support the main idea?

    a. _____

    b. _____

    c. _____

2. Where does the author put the most important idea?

    _____

SIGNAL WORDS

Remember that signal words help the reader understand your paragraph.

> **PARAGRAPH POINTER:** Adding New Ideas
>
> When you write paragraphs organized by order of importance, you should include signal words when you add a new supporting idea.

Study the list of signal words in the box.

ADDITION SIGNAL WORDS		
first	secondly	another (way, reason, example)
first of all	thirdly	also
for one thing	the most important (way, reason, example)	finally
		in addition
	most importantly	one (way, reason, example)
		the next (way, reason, example)

Activity 1

Underline the signal words in the paragraph "A Great Experience" on page 41.

Activity 2

Complete the following paragraph with signal words.

> Riding a bicycle can be a great alternative to driving a car. _____, you get a lot more exercise by riding a bicycle than by sitting behind the wheel of a car. _____, bicycles are less expensive than cars since they don't use gas and they cost less to repair. _____, bicycles are better for the environment because they don't cause pollution.

ORDERING SUPPORTING POINTS

Activity 1

1. Look at page 43. In a small group, discuss the topic "qualities of a good teacher."
2. Talk about the supporting points. Decide which one is the most important. Put a *1* in front of it. Decide the next most important point and put a *2* in front of it, and so on.
3. Use the list to complete the paragraph. Make sure you write the supporting points as complete sentences. You may begin with the most important idea or save it for last. Include signal words.
4. Follow the same steps for B and C.

A. Topic: qualities of a good teacher

Supporting Points

_____ has knowledge of subject

_____ cares about students

_____ can explain information clearly

A good teacher has several important qualities. First of all, a good teacher _____

_____

_____

_____

_____

B. Topic: things to consider when you choose a university

Supporting Points

_____ cost of attending the school

_____ location of the school

_____ quality of education

_____ number of students

There are four important things to consider when you choose a university. _____

_____

_____

_____

_____

C. Topic: how to do well in school

Supporting Points

_____ attend all classes

_____ take good notes

_____ complete all assignments

_____ study for exams in advance (don't cram)

There are several things you should do so that you will succeed in school. _____

_____

_____

_____

_____

Activity 2

For the next three paragraphs, discuss the topics and supporting points with your group. Write your own topic sentences. Number the supporting points in order of importance. Make sure you write the supporting points as complete sentences and use signal words.

A. Topic: difficult things about living in a foreign country

Supporting Points

_____ learning a new language

_____ adjusting to unfamiliar customs

_____ using different money

_____ feeling homesick

_____

_____

_____

_____

_____

B. Topic: benefits of a higher education

Supporting Points

_____ have more employment opportunities

_____ earn higher salary

_____ gain prestige

_____ learn valuable information

_____

_____

_____

_____

_____

C. Topic: how to make a good impression at a job interview

Supporting Points

_____ be on time

_____ come prepared

_____ ask questions

_____ be polite

_____ dress appropriately

_____

_____

_____

_____

_____

Activity 3

For the next three paragraphs, discuss the topic with your group and write your own supporting points. Number the items according to order of importance. Then write a paragraph based on your list. Remember to begin with a topic sentence and to include signal words.

A. Topic: things to consider when renting an apartment or buying a house

Supporting Points

____ _____

____ _____

____ _____

____ _____

_____

_____

_____

_____

_____

B. Topic: advantages of learning a foreign language

Supporting Points

_____   _____

_____   _____

_____   _____

_____   _____

_____

_____

_____

_____

_____

C. Topic: qualities of a good neighbor

Supporting Points

_____   _____

_____   _____

_____   _____

_____   _____

_____

_____

_____

_____

_____

GRAMMAR GUIDE: *WOULD RATHER*

We use the expression *would rather* to express preference. For example: "I would rather study in the library than at home." This statement means "I prefer to study in the library than study at home." Notice that *would rather* is followed by an infinitive verb without *to*.

Study the sentence structure with *would rather*.

AFFIRMATIVE SENTENCE	He would rather play a team sport than an individual sport.
NEGATIVE SENTENCE	I would rather not live in a dormitory.
QUESTION	Would you rather have dinner at a restaurant or eat at home?

WRITING PARAGRAPHS USING ORDER OF IMPORTANCE

A. Answer the following questions.

1. Would you rather live in a small town or a big city? _____

2. Which do you think is more important, luck or hard work? _____

3. Would you rather work for a large company or a small company? _____

B. Choose one of the questions from Exercise A to answer in a paragraph. Make a list of supporting points on the lines provided. Do not worry about the order.

Supporting Points

____ _____

____ _____

____ _____

____ _____

____ _____

C. Go over your list and cross out any items that do not belong. Then number the points in order of importance. Put a _1_ in front of the one you feel is the most important, and so on.

D. Write a topic sentence for your paragraph.

_____

E. Using the topic sentence and your list of supporting points, write a paragraph about your topic. You may begin with what you feel is the most important point or save it for last. Remember to use signal words.

_____

_____

_____

_____

_____

_____

_____

_____

EQUAL ORDER PARAGRAPHS

Sometimes you may feel that all of the points you are using as support are equally important. In this case, you list your points one by one. The order that you use is your choice.

Read the paragraph and answer the questions that follow. Notice that the author gives equal weight to each point.

Protecting Yourself From the Heat

There are several ways you can protect yourself when it gets very hot outside. One way is to avoid strenuous activity until the sun goes down. In addition, it is a good idea to wear lightweight and light-colored clothing. It is also important to drink a lot of water throughout the day so you don't get dehydrated. Finally, try to stay in the shade or in air-conditioned places.

1. What is the topic sentence? _____

   _____

2. How many supporting points does the author give? _____

Activity 1

A. **Have you ever thought about why trees are so important? Read the following list of valuable things that trees do for our planet. Discuss them with a partner.**

   - release oxygen into the air for animals to breathe
   - provide food and shelter for many animals
   - give us wood for building, fuel, and many other products
   - prevent soil from being washed away

B. **Can you think of one or two more reasons that trees are valuable?**

   _____   _____

C. **Complete the paragraph about the importance of trees. Use equal order to arrange the supporting points. Write a concluding sentence at the end of the paragraph.**

   Trees are very important to life on our planet. _____

   _____

   _____

   _____

   _____

   _____

   _____

Activity 2

A. Look at the agenda Martha Dickey prepared for a conference. After she sent out the agenda, she made several changes to the schedule. Now she needs to send an e-mail to her colleagues to notify them of the changes.

FLORIDA ADVERTISING GROUP

Spring Conference Agenda
April 25
Convention Center, Miami, Florida

Registration Deadline: ~~April 10~~ *March 30*

7:30 ~~7:00~~–8:30 A.M.	**Continental breakfast**	Main Lobby
8:30–9:00 A.M.	**Conference welcome and opening remarks**	Grand Ballroom B
9:00–10:15 A.M.	**Morning sessions**	
	New Frontiers: Marketing on Social Networking Sites	Conference Room 1
	Protecting Consumer Privacy	Conference Room 3
	Competition in Online Markets	Conference Room 4
10:15–10:45 A.M.	**Networking break**	Main Lobby
11:00–12:00 P.M.	**Keynote speaker Jason Keating**	
	Fast Forward: What's Next in Online Video Advertising?	Grand Ballroom
12:00–1:00 P.M.	**Lunch**	Conference Center Dining Hall A
1:00–2:30 P.M.	**Afternoon workshops**	*Conference Room 3*
	Measuring Success	~~Conference Room 2~~
	Web Marketing Techniques That Work	Conference Room 1
2:30–3:00 P.M.	**Networking break**	Main Lobby
3:00–5:00 P.M.	**Exhibitors display**	Second Floor Lobby
5:00–6:00 P.M.	**Closing remarks**	Grand Ballroom
7:30–10:00 ~~7:00–9:30~~ P.M.	**Dinner**	Sophie's Restaurant

B. **Write an e-mail that explains the changes to the schedule. Use signal words to introduce each change.**

Remember that e-mail messages are usually short and to the point. The subject line does not need to be a complete sentence, but it should identify the contents of the message.

| Send | Reply | Forward | Move | Print | Delete | ▲ | ▼ |

Subject: _____

From: _____

To: _____

_____

_____

_____

_____

_____

_____

_____

_____

_____

_____

_____

_____

Activity 3

A. **Choose one of the following topics to write about.**

- tips for staying healthy
- ways to impress your date
- things you like to do on the weekend
- qualities of a good friend

B. **Make a list of ideas to support the topic. Do not worry about the order.**

_____   _____

_____   _____

_____   _____

C. Go over your list and cross out any items that do not belong because they do not support the topic.

D. Write a topic sentence for your paragraph.

_____

E. Use the topic sentence and your list of supporting points to write a paragraph. You may put your supporting details in any order you choose. Remember to use signal words.

_____

_____

_____

_____

_____

_____

_____

YOU BE THE EDITOR

Read the paragraph. It contains nine mistakes. Correct the mistakes. Copy the corrected paragraph on a separate piece of paper.

Corn is one of the most important food sources on the world, but it have many another important uses as well. One of the most valuables uses of corn is as an alternative energy source. Ethanol, which is make from corn, is used to fuel cars and planes. some houses are even heated with ethanol fuel. Corn is also used to make plastics and fabrics. In fact, corn are used in thousands of products such as glue, shoe polish, aspirin, ink, and cosmetics. The syrup from corn sweetens Ice cream, soda, and candy. Scientists continue to researches new uses of corn and find more every year.

ON YOUR OWN

Write a paragraph about one of the following topics.
- qualities of a good/bad restaurant (hotel, school, etc.)
- qualities of a good/bad driver (or restaurant server, babysitter, taxi driver, etc.)

_____

_____

_____

When you describe a place, such as a room or a park, you organize the details according to their location. This is called spatial order. The easiest way to do this is to choose a starting point. Then describe where things are located in relation to your starting point. Decide on a logical method to follow, such as left to right, top to bottom, or front to back.

Read the paragraph. Choose the picture of the room that the paragraph describes. Put a check (✔) below that picture.

My Office

My home office is not very big, but it is comfortable and quiet. The light blue walls have a calming effect on me. There are big windows on the left wall, so the room is sunny and cheerful. I hung an amazing beaded tapestry from Thailand between the windows. My old oak desk fits perfectly under the two big windows. The desk once belonged to my grandfather. It's not in great condition, but it has sentimental value for me. Since my computer is on my desk, I can look out the window as I work. I have a wonderful view of the woods in back of my house, and I love looking at the trees. There is a small red suede couch on the back wall where my cat loves to take a nap while I am working. I have a bookcase on the right side of the couch and a file cabinet on the left side. There are several maps of places I have visited hanging on the wall to the right. Under the maps, I have a long narrow table with pictures of my family and friends on the top. The floor in the middle of the room is covered with a beautiful handmade rug I bought in Turkey. It has an intricate floral design. I really enjoy working in my office.

Notice that the topic sentence tells you the name of the place and something about it. The supporting sentences give details that describe the place. The concluding sentence gives a final thought about the place.

TOPIC SENTENCES FOR SPATIAL ORDER PARAGRAPHS

Write a topic sentence for each paragraph. In the topic sentence, mention the place being described and something about it.

1. _My bedroom is my favorite room in our house._ When you walk into the room, what you notice first are the large sliding glass doors to the left that open onto a balcony. My bed is opposite the balcony, on the wall to the right. When I sit in my bed I have a beautiful view of the garden. There is a painting above my bed that my great aunt did many years ago. I have a beautiful antique nightstand next to my bed on the right and a dresser on the left. On the back wall, there is a comfortable chair where I love to sit and read. Next to the chair is a small round table that is always covered with books and magazines. I love to spend time in my bedroom.

2. _____ My laptop computer is in the center where it is easy for me to reach. To the left of the computer, I keep a basket with pens, pencils, erasers, and paper clips. My calendar is right next to the basket. There is a small desk lamp in the right corner and a picture of my son next to it. It's very easy for me to work at my desk because everything is always in its place.

3. _____ In the center of the desk is a pile of old magazines and newspapers. The pile is growing every day. Next to that, there are several dirty coffee cups and a can of soda. There is a lamp in the left corner, but I use it to hold some baseball caps. An old box is on the right side of the desk. Inside the box are my bills and important papers. I also put receipts and letters in the box. The box is getting so full that soon I won't be able to put the top on it. I really should organize my desk soon.

4. _____ When you walk in the main entrance, the American art is on the first floor on your left. The Asian collection is directly in front of you, and the Islamic art is on your right. European paintings and sculptures are on the left side of the museum on the second floor. The Egyptian mummies and statues are on the opposite side of the museum on the second floor. The Greek and Roman statues are on the left side of the third floor. Finally, the African collection is on the right side. When you leave the museum, you feel like you've seen something from almost every part of the world.

5. _____ As you walk up the central grand staircase that leads to the first-floor lobby you will feel enchanted. The whole lobby has beautiful thick red carpeting and wood paneled walls. In the center of the lobby, there is an exquisite crystal chandelier hanging from the ceiling. Under that sits a large round antique table with a vase full of fresh flowers. Around the table there are a few elegant, but comfortable leather sofas and chairs for people to relax in. To the right of the table, there is a baby grand piano. There are more chairs and small tables behind the piano in an area that opens onto a lovely garden. A local musician plays soft jazz for the guests having afternoon tea. On the far right of the lobby is a long desk. Behind the desk there are usually several people checking people in and out of the hotel. Finally, in the far left corner of the lobby across from the front desk, there is a small gift shop.

GRAMMAR GUIDE: PREPOSITIONS OF PLACE

Prepositions of place are often used as signal words to show position or location.

A. Study the words in the chart.

PREPOSITIONS OF PLACE			
across	in back of	on	outside
at	in front of	on both sides	over
at the end	in the center	on the end	under
behind	in the middle	on the left	
beside	inside	on the right	
between	next to	on top of	

B. Study the floor plan of Lourie's Department Store. Then read the paragraph that follows on page 55. Notice that the paragraph is organized by space order. Underline the prepositions of place.

LOURIE'S
FIRST FLOOR

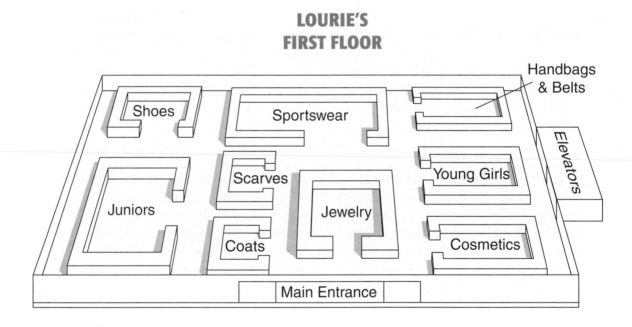

The first floor of Lourie's sells clothing and accessories for women. As you enter the store through the main entrance, the jewelry department is directly in front of you in the middle of the store. The coat department is on the left and the cosmetics department is on the right. The juniors shop is on the left, next to coats. Women's shoes are located in the left rear corner. Next to the shoe department, behind jewelry, is the sportswear department. Handbags and belts are next to sportswear in the right rear corner. The young girls department is on the right, between handbags and cosmetics. The elevators are on the right wall.

C. **Look at the picture of the jewelry department and complete the following sentences with the correct prepositions.**

1. The customers are standing _____ the counter.

2. The jewelry is _____ the case.

3. The little girl is standing _____ her parents.

4. The saleswoman is _____ the counter.

5. There is a mirror _____ the counter.

6. The sale sign is _____ the saleswoman.

Activity 1

A. **Complete the floor plan of the second floor of Lourie's using the information in the sentences.**

LOURIE'S
SECOND FLOOR

1. When you get off the elevator, the men's casual clothing department is to the left.
2. Men's shoes are to the right of the elevator.
3. The coat and suit department are straight ahead in the middle of the store.
4. Shirts and sweaters are behind the coat and suit department in the left corner.
5. The ties are in the right corner, next to the shirts and sweaters.

B. **Complete the paragraph describing the second floor. Use spatial order to organize the information.**

The second floor of Lourie's has all the clothing a man needs. When you get off the

elevator, _____

_____

_____

_____

_____

_____

_____

_____

_____

_____

Write a paragraph describing the third floor based on the following floor plan. Use spatial order to organize the information. Begin with a topic sentence and use signal words.

LOURIE'S
THIRD FLOOR

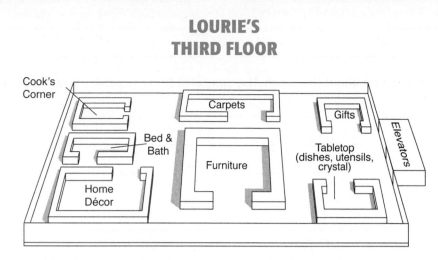

_____

_____

_____

_____

_____

PARAGRAPH POINTER: Organizing Details

There are several ways to organize details in a descriptive paragraph. For example, you may start on the left side and move right, go from right to left, or from top to bottom. Choose the pattern that best suits your topic, and then stick to that pattern throughout the paragraph.

Activity 3

A. Draw a simple picture of one of the following: a room in your house, apartment, or dormitory; a hotel room; your office or classroom.

B. **Make a list of the things in the room such as furniture, lights, rugs, artwork, and windows.**

_____   _____

_____   _____

_____   _____

C. **Write a paragraph about the room. Use spatial order to organize your information.**

_____

_____

_____

_____

_____

_____

_____

D. **After you have written your paragraph, find a partner. Ask him or her to read your paragraph and draw a picture of the room based on your description.**

E. **Compare your picture and your partner's picture of the room. Are there any differences? If yes, discuss them with your partner. Can you think of ways to make your paragraph clearer? Copy your revised paragraph on a separate piece of paper.**

Activity 4

Imagine that your school is putting on a production of a play you wrote. You need to write a description of the stage set. Draw a picture of the set. Use the picture to write a description of the set.

_____

_____

_____

_____

_____

_____

Activity 5

Use the map of the United States to complete the paragraph that follows.

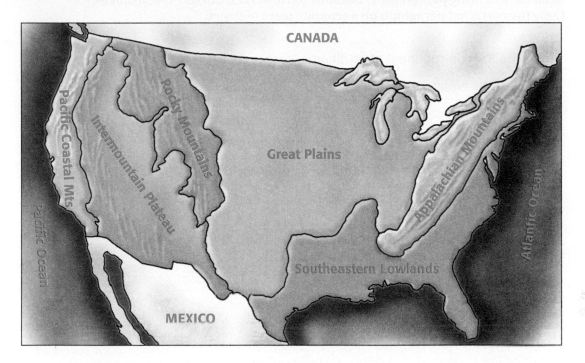

The United States is a large country in North America bordered by Canada to the north and Mexico to the south. The Atlantic Ocean lies to the east and the Pacific Ocean lies to the west. The United States has six very different regions. _____

_____

_____

_____

_____

_____

_____

_____

_____

YOU BE THE EDITOR

Read the following paragraph. It contains ten mistakes. Correct the mistakes. Copy the corrected paragraph on a separate piece of paper.

The triangle continent of south america is quite large. It stretches from north of the equator down nearly to the Antarctic Circle. South America has three differents kinds of landscapes. in the west, the magnificent andes Mountains rise all along the whole pacific ocean coast. They extend along the entire continent from northern to south. There are rainforests in the Amazon valley and along the Caribbean coast that cover most of the north and northeast. In the south are the grasslands and pampas that go down to the rocky point at the bottom of the continent called Cape Horn.

ON YOUR OWN

Use spatial order to write a paragraph about one of the following places.
- a doctor's office
- a garden
- the view out your window
- a student lounge
- your kitchen

UNDERSTANDING THE WRITING PROCESS

Even the best writers rarely compose a perfect piece of writing on the first try. They understand that writing is a process. In this chapter you will practice the basic steps in the writing process.

Copyright 2004 by Randy Glasbergen.
www.glasbergen.com

WHY ARE WE DOING THIS?

"It's not a great mission statement, but we'll revise it if things get better."

THE WRITING PROCESS

Writing is a process that involves several steps: prewriting, writing, and revising.

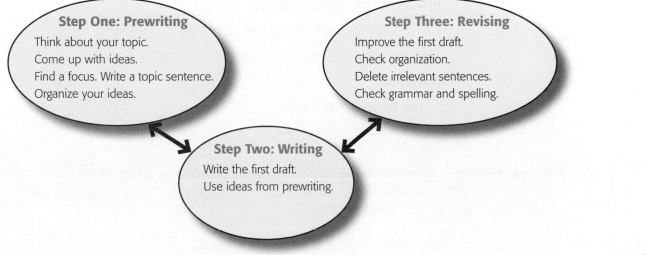

Step One: Prewriting
Think about your topic.
Come up with ideas.
Find a focus. Write a topic sentence.
Organize your ideas.

Step Three: Revising
Improve the first draft.
Check organization.
Delete irrelevant sentences.
Check grammar and spelling.

Step Two: Writing
Write the first draft.
Use ideas from prewriting.

STEP ONE: PREWRITING

Prewriting is the thinking, talking, reading, and organizing you do before you write a first draft. Prewriting is a way of warming up your brain before you write, just as you warm up your body before you exercise. There are several ways to warm up before you write.

Brainstorming

Brainstorming is a quick way to generate a lot of ideas on a topic. The purpose is to make a list of as many ideas as possible without worrying about how you will use them. Your list can include words, phrases, sentences, or even questions. Then you use your list to come up with a specific focus for a paragraph.

A. **To brainstorm, follow these steps:**

1. Begin with a general topic and write down as many ideas about the topic as you can in five minutes.

2. Add more items to your list by answering the questions *What?*, *How?*, *When?*, *Where?*, *Why?*, and *Who?*

3. Look over your list. Group similar items on the list together.

4. Look for a focus in one of the groups and write a topic sentence.

5. Cross out items that do not belong.

B. **Look at the following example of brainstorming on the topic of TV commercials.**

> ## TV Commercials
>
> Favorites
>
> Kinds of commercials
>
> BORING!
>
> Car commercials are my favorites
>
> Funny ones
>
> See new products
>
> Racist and sexist
>
> Too many
>
> Interrupt the flow of shows
>
> Food commercials make me hungry
>
> Use famous people to promote products
>
> Annoying
>
> Some have good music
>
> Bad for kids

You can brainstorm ideas by yourself or with a group of people. You already did some brainstorming with your classmates in Chapter 2, when you made a list of ideas about the topic "It is difficult to learn a new language."

Activity 1

A. **Work in a small group. Choose one person to be the secretary. Pick one of the following topics to brainstorm with your group.**
- friends
- travel
- education

B. **Brainstorm ideas about the topic your group chose. Each member must contribute ideas to the list. The secretary should write a list of all the ideas on a separate piece of paper.**

C. **Read over your list. Organize your list by grouping similar ideas together. Cross out items that do not belong.**

D. **Look for a focus and write a topic sentence for a paragraph.**

E. **Write your topic sentence on the board and discuss all the topic sentences as a class.**

Activity 2

A. **Choose one of the following topics to brainstorm.**
- jobs
- movies
- vacations

B. **Follow the steps for brainstorming on a separate piece of paper.**

C. **Share your topic sentence with several of your classmates.**

Clustering

Clustering is another prewriting technique. It is a visual way of showing how your ideas are connected using circles and lines. When you use this technique, you draw a diagram of your ideas.

A. **To cluster, follow these steps:**

1. Write your topic in the center of a blank piece of paper and draw a circle around it.
2. Write any ideas that come into your mind about the topic in circles around the main circle.
3. Connect these ideas to the center word with a line.
4. Think about each of your new ideas, and make more circles around it.
5. Repeat this process until you run out of ideas.
6. Look at your cluster diagram. You can see which ideas go together. Write a topic sentence.

B. Look at the example of a cluster diagram on the topic of television commercials.

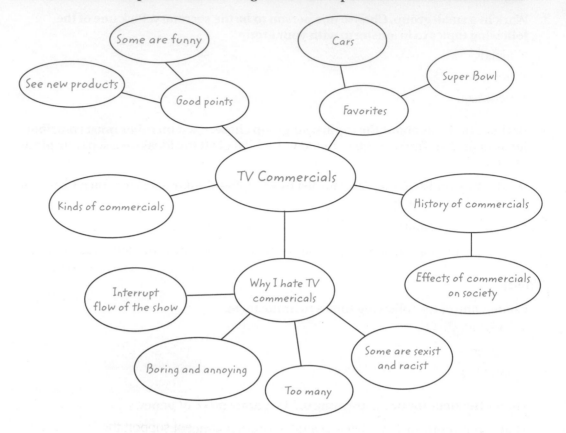

Activity 1

A. Choose one of the following topics. Write the topic in the middle of a piece of paper and follow steps 1–5 for making a cluster diagram.

- sports
- health
- music

B. Look at your cluster diagram. Choose an aspect of the topic that you like and that you have enough ideas to write a paragraph about. Write a topic sentence for that paragraph.

Organizing Your Ideas

After you have spent some time thinking about your topic and doing some prewriting exercises, you are ready to organize your information. One of the easiest ways to organize your ideas is to make a simple list or outline. Put the ideas in the order that you plan to use when you write. You can use the list or outline as a guide while you are writing. Remember that the list or outline is not permanent. You may discover new ideas or discard some ideas as you are writing.

Look at the following example of a simple outline.

Example:

I dislike TV commercials for several reasons.

1. are too long and boring
2. interrupt the flow of the show
3. are racist and sexist
4. have a bad influence on children

STEP TWO: WRITING

Now you are ready to write the first draft of your paragraph. When you write the first draft of your paragraph, use the ideas you generated from prewriting and your outline or list.

As you write the first draft, don't worry about producing a perfect paragraph. Use the chart below to help you.

PARAGRAPH POINTER: Writing First Drafts

When you write the first draft:

- begin with a topic sentence that states the main idea
- include several sentences that support the main idea
- stick to the topic—do not include information that does not support the main idea
- organize the sentences so that the order of ideas makes sense
- use signal words to help the reader understand how the ideas in your paragraph are connected
- end with a concluding sentence if appropriate

Practice writing the first draft of a paragraph. Choose one of the topics you used in the brainstorming or clustering activity.

_____

_____

_____

_____

_____

_____

_____

_____

_____

_____

STEP THREE: REVISING

Do not think of the first draft as a final product. After you write the first draft, you should look for ways to improve it. This is called revising. When you revise, you can add new ideas to support the topic. You can also delete irrelevant sentences. If the supporting sentences are not in a logical order, you should rearrange them. Finally, you should check your paragraph for any mistakes in grammar, punctuation, and spelling.

A. **Use the Revising Checklist to revise your paragraphs.**

REVISING CHECKLIST	YES	NO
1. Does the topic sentence include a topic and a controlling idea?		
2. Do all of the supporting sentences relate to the main idea?		
3. Are the sentences in the right order?		
4. Is there enough support for the topic sentence?		
5. Are there signal words to help guide the reader?		
6. Is the punctuation, spelling, and grammar correct?		

Revising Activity

B. **Read the paragraphs. Use the Revising Checklist to help you make revisions. After reading, add the sentence that follows to the paragraph. Draw an asterisk (*) where it should be inserted.**

1. My little brother, Tim, has several annoying habits. For one thing, he follows me everywhere. He is like my shadow. I enjoy my privacy, but because of Tim, I am never alone. His most annoying habit is eating with his mouth open. I feel sick when I have lunch with him. I hope he learns some table manners soon. Tommy has curly red hair, just like me. Another problem is that Tommy leaves his toys all over the house. I am always tripping on his toy cars or trucks. The house is always a mess with Tim around.

   _____

   _____

   _____

   _____

   _____

   _____

   _____

   _____

   _____

   _____

   He even follows me into the bathroom.

2.   Every year my school has a talent show to raise money for new books for the library. This year I was the host. The show was amazing and everyone involved did a great job. One group of students formed a band and played three popular songs. My favorite act, however, was definitely my friend Ben's magic show. Ben is also a good student. He did about ten tricks that no one in the audience could figure out. There were also some nice dance performances and a comedy act that left the audience crying from laughing so much. With the help of all the great performers and, of course, the audience who came to see the show, we raised close to $5,000.

_____

_____

_____

_____

_____

_____

_____

_____

_____

That can buy a lot of new books!

3.   Some fast food restaurants from Asia are providing diners with a healthier alternative to the usual choices of burgers and fries. For example, a Korean food chain, Sorabol, is bringing traditional Korean cuisine to fast food venues in the United States. Unlike most American fast food that is pre-made and then delivered to the store, Sorabol's food is prepared every day, so you know the ingredients are fresh. Lots of fast food restaurants offer many kinds of pizza. Sorabol is a family-owned chain, and the owners pride themselves on offering a clean, casual, inexpensive dining experience to fit today's fast-paced society. With restaurants already established in West Coast cities such as San Francisco and Seattle, Sorabol is planning on expanding across the country as its popularity increases. Hopefully we can all enjoy Korean BBQ take-out over the next couple of years!

_____

_____

_____

_____

_____

_____

_____

_____

_____

In fact, plans are already underway to expand to Washington, D.C., and New York City.

4. My friends and I love to read so much that we started our own book club. At the beginning of each month, one member of the club selects a book for us to read. That person sends an e-mail to everyone with the title and author of the book. She is also responsible for hosting a small party on the last Monday of each month when we all get together to have dinner and discuss the book. The person who chooses the book changes each month, which is great because I get to read and discuss all different types of books. For example, last month we read a mystery my friend Beth recommended. I met Beth last year at work. This month, we are reading a biography of Abraham Lincoln. Next month, it's my turn to pick a book. Book clubs are a great way to keep reading and do something fun with your friends.

_____

_____

_____

_____

_____

_____

_____

_____

I'll probably pick a romance novel by Marianne Lewis, my favorite author.

GRAMMAR GUIDE: SENTENCE FRAGMENTS

Every English sentence must have a subject and a verb. It must also express a complete thought. If a sentence lacks a subject or a verb or is not a complete thought, it is called a fragment. Check your writing to make sure you do not have any sentence fragments.

A. **There are three common kinds of fragments. Study the chart.**

PROBLEMS	EXAMPLES/SOLUTIONS
no subject	Fragment: Wrote a paragraph about friendship. Complete sentence: Allie wrote a paragraph about friendship.
no verb	Fragment: The whole team, as well as the fans. Complete sentence: The whole team, as well as the fans, ran onto the field.
not a complete thought	Fragment: As soon as I fell asleep. Complete sentence: As soon as I fell asleep, the phone rang.

B. **Write *C* in front of each complete sentence. Write *F* in front of each sentence fragment. Then, rewrite the fragments so that they are complete sentences.**

_F_ 1. After I got home from a long day at the office.

After I got home from a long day at the office, I was too tired to make dinner.

_____ 2. Mr. Steven's older brother and sister.

_____

_____ 3. The roads are slippery from the rain, so drive carefully and keep your lights on.

_____

_____ 4. Under the table where the cat usually hides.

_____

_____ 5. To apply for a scholarship at the University of Pennsylvania.

_____

_____ 6. Two young men from different cities met on a train going to Paris.

_____

_____ 7. Because I knew it would be too expensive to fly there.

_____

_____ 8. Has been painted several times over the years.

_____

Read the situation and write a paragraph.

Situation: Your friend has just moved to a new place and is having trouble meeting new people. You are writing him or her a note of encouragement. You want to give some tips about how to make new friends.

Writing Exercise 1

Prewriting

A. Brainstorm a list (or make a cluster diagram) of ideas about how to make new friends. Use a separate piece of paper.

B. Share your ideas with a partner. Add some new ideas. Cross out any ideas that are not related to the main idea.

C. Write a topic sentence.

_____

Writing

Write the first draft of your paragraph. Use your prewriting as a guide. Begin with your topic sentence and organize your sentences in a logical order.

_____

_____

_____

_____

_____

_____

Revising

A. Read your paragraph. Try to improve it. Use the Revising Checklist on page 66.

_____

_____

_____

_____

_____

_____

_____

B. Correct the grammar, spelling, and punctuation. Copy your revised paragraph on a separate piece of paper.

Writing Exercise 2

Read the situation and write a paragraph. Complete the steps of the writing process with a partner.

Situation: You are writing an article about international students for your local newspaper. You want to include a paragraph about your partner.

Prewriting

A. **Ask and answer the questions with a partner. Write the answers on the lines.**

Your partner's name: _____

1. Where are you from?

    _____

2. What is your native language?

    _____

3. Do you know any other languages?

    _____

4. Why are you learning English?

    _____

5. Have you visited any other countries? If so, which ones?

    _____

B. **Write three more questions to ask your partner. You can ask questions about your partner's:**
   - job/education
   - hobbies
   - family

1. question: _____

    answer: _____

2. question: _____

    answer: _____

3. question: _____

    answer: _____

C. **Write a topic sentence about your partner.**

_____

Writing

Write the first draft of a paragraph about your partner. Use the information from your partner's answers as a guide.

_____

_____

_____

_____

_____

_____

_____

Revising

A. Ask your partner to read your paragraph. Does he or she have any suggestions? Write down your partner's suggestions. You can also use the Revising Checklist on page 66 to help you.

B. Correct the grammar, spelling, and punctuation. Copy your revised paragraph on a separate piece of paper.

YOU BE THE EDITOR

Read the paragraph. It contains eight mistakes. Correct the mistakes. Copy the corrected paragraph on a separate piece of paper.

> There are several thing you can do to enhance your performance on an exam. First, Make sure to get a good night's sleep the night before the test. that means sleeping for at least eight hour. It is also important to eat a good breakfast the morning of the exam, so You won't have hungry during the exam Finally, bring a bottle of water to the test in case you got thirsty. Just don't drink too much, or you may have to get up in the middle of the exam for a bathroom break.

ON YOUR OWN

Choose one of the topics on pages 63 and 64 that you did not already write about. Write a paragraph on the topic. Practice the steps of prewriting, writing, and revising. Remember to use the Revising Checklist on page 66.

SUPPORTING THE MAIN IDEA

You have learned that a paragraph is a group of sentences about one main idea that is stated in a topic sentence. You have also learned that a paragraph needs sentences with supporting details to develop the main idea.

Supporting details can come from many places, such as your own personal experience, examples, quotes, or facts. In this chapter, you will learn more about how to support a main idea.

ADDING ADDITIONAL DETAILS

As you begin to write longer, more developed paragraphs, you will need to add details to your main supporting points. This will make your paragraphs more complete.

Activity 1

A. **Read the following paragraph about reducing stress. It has a topic sentence, three supporting sentences, and a concluding sentence.**

> I do several things to reduce my stress during final exams. First of all, I exercise every day. In addition, I am more careful about my diet. Finally, I take breaks while I am studying. All of these things help me through the stressful week of finals.

B. **Read this revised paragraph. Now each major supporting point is followed by additional details that provide more information.**

I do several things to reduce my stress during final exams. First of all, I exercise every day. I try to do at least thirty minutes of aerobic exercise such as riding my bike or jogging. Exercising helps me focus on something else, and it makes me feel better. In addition, I am more careful about my diet during finals. I avoid foods that are high in sugar because they make me jittery, and I stay away from fatty foods because they make me tired. I try to eat well-balanced meals and healthy snacks such as fruit and nuts. Finally, I take breaks while I am studying. Every few hours, I do something enjoyable such as watch my favorite TV show, call my friends, or listen to music. I relax during my breaks and feel more energized when I go back to studying. All of these things help me through the stressful week of finals.

C. **Complete the simple outline based on the paragraph you've just read.**

Topic sentence: I do several things to reduce my stress during final exams.

Main supporting point 1: _I exercise every day._

Detail: _I do thirty minutes of aerobic exercise such as riding my bike or jogging._

Detail: _____

Main supporting point 2: _____

Detail: _____

Detail: _____

Main supporting point 3: _____

Detail: _____

Detail: _____

Activity 2

Complete the paragraph by adding specific details to strengthen each main supporting point.

There are several ways to save money on your monthly expenses. First of all, you can spend less money on food. _____

_____

_____

You can also economize on entertainment. _____

_____

_____

Finally, you can save money on rent. _____

_____

USING EXAMPLES FOR SUPPORT

Writers often use examples to support topic sentences and main supporting points. In fact, examples are one of the best ways to help readers understand your ideas.

Read the paragraph. Underline the examples.

My cousin Alex loves to collect things. For example, he has an amazing stamp collection. He started collecting stamps about ten years ago and now he has some very rare and valuable ones. He keeps all of his stamps neatly arranged in special leather albums. Alex also collects coins from all around the world. He recently told me he had coins from more than 100 countries. In addition, Alex collects some more unusual things such as antique toys and old model airplanes. He arranges them in display cases around his apartment. According to Alex, collecting things can be very educational. For instance, he has learned a lot about the history of certain places in the process of collecting stamps and coins. Last but not least, Alex seems to collect people. I have never met anyone with so many friends.

GRAMMAR GUIDE: *FOR EXAMPLE, FOR INSTANCE, SUCH AS*

The phrases *for example* and *for instance* are used at the beginning of a complete sentence. Use a comma after the phrase.

The phrase *such as* is used to introduce short examples within a sentence. Commas are usually not necessary.

PHRASE	EXAMPLES
for example	Martha enjoys outdoor sports. **For example**, she loves snowboarding and skiing.
for instance	My computer has lots of problems. **For instance**, it freezes almost once a day.
such as	I prefer to wear clothes made out of natural fibers **such as** cotton, silk, and wool.

A. Read each statement. Then choose an example from the box to support each statement. Write the appropriate example on the lines following the statement. Remember to begin the example with the phrase *for example* or *for instance* and to use a comma.

1. Are you bored with your job? If so, there are plenty of unusual jobs to help make working more pleasurable for you. _____

   _____

2. Some people believe that dreams can indicate future events. _____

   _____

3. In addition to shoes that make a fashion statement, there are many different kinds of shoes for special purposes. _____

   _____

> **There are special shoes for playing soccer, tap dancing, hiking, and bowling.**
>
> **A furniture tester actually gets paid to sit in chairs and sofas and make sure the furniture is comfortable before it is sold to the public.**
>
> **In some cultures, a dream of a rainbow is believed to predict eventual good fortune.**

B. Complete the sentences.

1. Some colors such as _____ and _____ have a soothing effect on me.

2. Games such as _____ and _____ are fun to watch.

3. Exercises such as _____ and _____ are good for your heart.

4. Some of my friends such as _____ and _____ are good listeners.

5. Several planets such as _____ and _____ have at least one moon.

WRITING PARAGRAPHS WITH EXAMPLES

Writing Exercise 1

Prewriting

A. Write two or three examples for each statement.

1. Several inventions have dramatically changed the way people live.

   _____

   _____

2. In my culture, there are certain things that are considered impolite.

_____

_____

3. Recycling is an easy, but important, way to help the planet.

_____

_____

B. **Discuss your examples in a small group.**

C. **Choose one of the statements to use as a topic sentence for a paragraph. Use your examples as the main supporting points. Add details to strengthen these points. Make a simple outline before you write.**

Topic sentence: _____

Main supporting point 1: _____

Detail: _____

Detail: _____

Main supporting point 2: _____

Detail: _____

Detail: _____

Main supporting point 3: _____

Detail: _____

Detail: _____

Writing

Write your first draft. Use the expressions *for example, for instance,* and *such as*.

_____

_____

_____

_____

_____

_____

_____

_____

_____

_____

_____

Revising

A. **Look for ways to improve your paragraph. Use the Revising Checklist on page 66. Also think about these questions as you revise your paragraph.**

1. Are all of your examples relevant?

2. Did you add details for the main supporting points?

3. Did you use the expressions *for example, for instance,* and *such as* correctly?

B. **Check for errors in grammar, spelling, and punctuation. Copy your revised paragraph on a separate piece of paper.**

Writing Exercise 2

Prewriting

People learn in different ways. Some people learn by reading about things. Other people learn by doing things. Still others learn by listening to people talk about things. Discuss these learning styles in small groups. Make a list or outline before you begin to write.

A. **Think about the different ways people learn.**

B. **Which of these ways is most effective for you?** _____

C. **Make a list of examples that support your answer.**

Writing

Write the first draft of a paragraph about how you learn new information best. Use specific examples to support your answer.

_____

_____

_____

_____

_____

_____

_____

_____

_____

Revising

A. **Exchange papers with a partner. Look for ways to improve your partner's paragraph. Do the examples support the topic sentence? Give your partner some advice.**

B. **Correct your partner's grammar, spelling, and punctuation.**

C. **Read the suggestions your partner gave you. Decide which of these suggestions you will use. Make your changes. Copy your revised paragraph on a separate piece of paper.**

Follow-up Activity

A. **Interview each of your classmates. Find out what way each of them learns best. Then complete the chart about learning styles in your class.**

LEARNING STYLE	NUMBER OF PEOPLE
Learn best by reading about things	
Learn best by doing things	
Learn best by listening to people talk about things	

B. **Write a paragraph about the different learning styles in your class.**

Writing Exercise 3

Prewriting

A. **Many things influence young adults. Which do you think has more influence—family, friends, or media? Discuss this with your classmates.**

B. **Find several people who agree with you. On a separate sheet of paper, make a list of examples to support your idea.**

Writing

Work together to write a paragraph. Use your examples.

_____

_____

_____

_____

_____

_____

_____

_____

Revising

A. **Look for ways to improve your group's paragraph.**

1. Are all of your examples relevant?

2. Can you add any more examples?

B. **Check for errors in grammar, spelling, and punctuation. Copy your revised paragraph on a separate piece of paper.**

Follow-up Activity

Find a group that has a different position and exchange paragraphs. Read each other's paragraphs and discuss the question again. Do you still have the same opinion?

USING A PERSONAL EXPERIENCE FOR SUPPORT

Writing about a personal experience is another effective way to support a topic sentence.

Read the paragraph. Then answer the questions.

> Sometimes a stranger can be a real friend. The woman I met on my way home from work yesterday is a perfect example. I left my office late and forgot that my car needed gas. I had been driving on the expressway for about ten minutes when the car started making strange noises. Then it suddenly stopped. I was out of gas, and I was scared because it was getting dark. After a few minutes, a young couple stopped and offered to help me. They went to a gas station, bought a big can of gas, and put the gas in my tank. The woman told me that when she saw me looking so alone and upset, she told her husband to stop. She wanted to help me because she hoped that someone would stop and help her in a similar situation.

1. What is the topic sentence?

   _____

2. How are the supporting sentences organized?

   _____

3. What is the concluding sentence?

   _____

4. The ideas in the paragraph are organized by time order. What words signal time order? Do you think the student's experience supports her topic sentence?

   _____

Writing Exercise 1

Prewriting

A. **Discuss these expressions with your teacher and classmates. What do they mean?**
   - Money is the root of all evil.
   - Two heads are better than one.
   - Variety is the spice of life.
   - Haste makes waste.
   - Don't count your chickens before they hatch.
   - Too many cooks spoil the broth.

B. **Choose one expression to write about. Think of an experience from your own life that proves or disproves the expression. Tell a partner about your experience.**

Writing

Complete the paragraph with a personal experience. Organize your ideas according to time order. Use the phrases on page 75 to connect your ideas.

The expression, "_____"

(is usually / is not always) true. _____

_____

_____

_____

_____

_____

_____

Revising

A. Read over the paragraph you wrote. Look for ways to improve it. Use the Revising Checklist on page 66 to help you. As you revise, think about these questions.

1. Are the sentences in correct time order?

2. Did you include signal words?

3. Did you include a concluding sentence?

B. Check for errors in grammar, spelling, and punctuation. Copy your revised paragraph on a separate piece of paper.

Writing Exercise 2

Prewriting

A. Discuss these statements in small groups.

- Good things happen when you least expect them.
- Sometimes hard work is not rewarded.
- Things often don't turn out the way you planned.

B. Think of an experience in your life that supports one of the statements. Make a list of the events in your experience. Use time order.

_____   _____

_____   _____

_____   _____

C. Write a topic sentence for your paragraph.

_____

Writing

Use your list to write the first draft of the paragraph supporting the statement you chose.

_____

_____

_____

_____

_____

_____

_____

_____

_____

_____

Revising

A. Read the paragraph you wrote. Look for ways to improve it. Use the Revising Checklist on page 66 to help you.

B. Check for errors in grammar, spelling, and punctuation. Copy your revised paragraph on a separate piece of paper.

USING FACTS AND STATISTICS FOR SUPPORT

Writers often use facts and statistics to support their main idea. A fact is something you know to be true because it exists, has happened, or can be proven. Statistics are facts presented as numbers.

A. Read the paragraph a student wrote. Underline the facts and statistics that support the main idea.

> Last summer I rode the Trans-Siberian Railroad, the longest continuous rail line in the world. It actually crosses the whole Russian Federation. I boarded the train in the capital, Moscow, and rode 5,870 miles (9,446 kilometers) to the Pacific port of Vladivostok. It was a long ride, but I wasn't bored at all. The whole journey took eight days to complete. During that time, I met lots of interesting people. We crossed eight times zones along the way. It was a long trip but well worth it.

B. Read the newspaper article. Underline the facts and statistics that support the main idea.

Iowa under Water

One of the worst storms in recent history caused widespread flooding throughout the state of Iowa last weekend. By Friday, nine of Iowa's rivers were above historic flood levels. In Iowa's second largest city, Cedar Rapids, the Cedar River rose to 32 feet. That's 12 feet higher than the previous record, which was set in 1929. More than 400 city blocks and 3,900 homes were left underwater. In Iowa's capital, Des Moines, floodwaters from the Des Moines River poured through the city breaking the levees. By Monday, more than 36,000 Iowans had left their homes, and the governor declared disaster areas in 83 of Iowa's 99 counties. State officials estimate that damage from this storm will cost at least $737 million. The floods destroyed about 20 percent of Iowa's overall grain crop and damaged more than one million acres of corn.

C. Read the paragraph from a brochure about the Great Smoky Mountains National Park. Underline the facts and statistics that support the main idea.

The Great Smoky Mountains National Park is the home of a huge variety of plant and animal life. For example, there are more than 10,000 species of plants—including 130 different kinds of trees—growing in the park. That is more than in any other North American national park. There are also 1,600 flowering plant species and at least 4,000 species of non-flowering plants that live in the park. In addition, more than 200 types of birds, 66 types of mammals, and 50 native fish species make their home in the Great Smoky Mountains National Park. Another interesting fact is that more species of salamanders can be found there than anywhere else on our planet.

Writing Exercise

Prewriting

Look at the photo. Discuss it with a partner. Have you ever seen an ostrich? What do you know about ostriches?

Writing

Write a paragraph about ostriches. Use facts from the list to support the topic sentence. Choose facts from the list that support the topic sentence.

Topic sentence: Ostriches, the largest and strongest birds in the world, are unusual animals.

Facts:

* It cannot fly but is the fastest two-legged animal on the planet; it can run up to 40 miles (65 kilometers) an hour for 30 minutes.
* It is the only bird that has 2 toes on each foot; all other birds have 3 or 4 toes.
* average height: 2.4 meters tall (about 8 feet)
* average weight: up to 136 kilograms (300 pounds)
* It has feathers like all other birds.
* Females can lay from 10 to 70 eggs each year.
* It lays the largest bird egg, weighing about 3 pounds (1.4 kilograms) and measuring between 6 and 8 inches (about 15–20 centimeters) long.
* Females lay more eggs at one time than any other bird—up to 15.

_____

_____

_____

_____

_____

_____

_____

_____

_____

Revising

A. Read the paragraph you wrote. Look for ways to improve it. Use the Revising Checklist on page 66 to help you.

B. Check for errors in grammar, spelling, and punctuation. Copy your revised paragraph on a separate piece of paper.

Facts and statistics are often presented in graphs, tables, and charts. Sometimes you will need to describe this information and use it as support. The words in the boxes will help you describe changes shown on a graph, table, or chart.

VERBS THAT DESCRIBE CHANGE				
climb	decrease	fall	increase	remain the same
decline	drop	fluctuate	level off	rise

ADJECTIVES AND ADVERBS DESCRIBING AMOUNT OF CHANGE			
dramatic	sharp	slightly	steady
gradual	slight	small	sudden

Activity 1

Look at the graph. Work with a partner. Write four sentences about the average age of men at first marriage and on page 86, write five sentences about the average age of women at first marriage. Use a variety of words from the box.

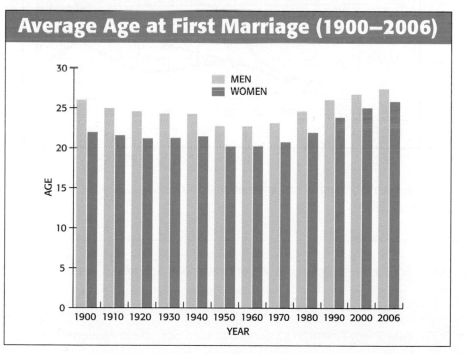

Average Age at First Marriage (1900–2006)

Men

1. <u>The average age of men at first marriage fell between 1900 and 1950.</u>

2. _____

3. _____

4. _____

5. _____

Women

1. _____

2. _____

3. _____

4. _____

5. _____

Activity 2

A. **Look at the graph and answer the questions that follow. The name of the graph tells you what kind of information is presented.**

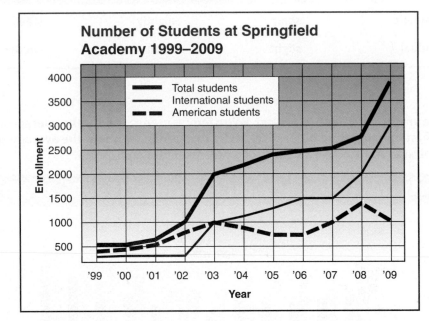

Number of Students at Springfield Academy 1999–2009

1. In what year was the number of international students equal to the number of American students?

   _____

2. In 2003, how many international students attended Springfield Academy?

   _____

3. In 2001, how many American students attended Springfield Academy?

   _____

4. In what years did the number of American students remain the same?

   _____

5. In what years did the number of international students remain the same?

_____

6. When did enrollment of international students reach 2000?

_____

7. In what year were there twice as many international students as American students?

_____

B. **Read the situation. Use specific information from the graph to write the part of the paragraph that describes the student body.**

Situation: You are an international student at Springfield Academy, and you feel that there should be more social and cultural activities for international students. Since the number of international students is growing every year, you believe that the school has a responsibility to help them socially and culturally as well as academically.

> Since the number of international students at Springfield Academy is
> growing every year, the school needs to organize more social and cultural
> activities for us. In the past, this may not have been so important, but today
> things are different. In 1999, _____
>
> _____
>
> _____
>
> _____
>
> _____
>
> _____
>
> _____
>
> _____
>
> _____
>
> _____
>
> _____

Because international students now represent such a large percentage of the student body, I believe that the school has a responsibility to help us outside the classroom. For example, I would like the school to organize sightseeing tours around the city. It would also be a good idea to arrange visits with American families. I'm sure all the other international students would agree with me.

Writing Exercise 1

Prewriting

Look at the chart and answer the questions to help you write a report.

Percentage Distribution of International Students in U.S. by Major Fields

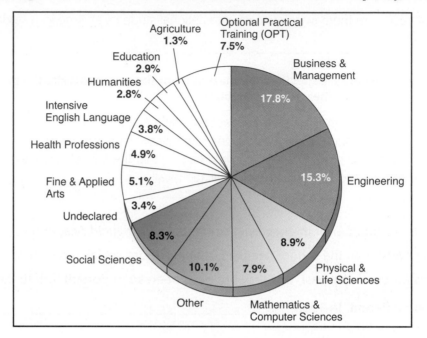

1. What is the most popular field? _____

2. What percentage of international students are studying engineering? _____

3. What is the second most popular field? _____

4. What percentage is studying business and management? _____

5. This means that _____ percent of all international students are studying either engineering or business and management.

6. This is followed by _____ percent studying physical and life sciences and _____ percent studying social sciences.

7. What are some other fields that international students study? _____

   _____

Writing

Read the situation. Complete the paragraph from the report. Support the topic sentence with facts from the chart.

Situation: You are opening an English language school. You have to write a report describing the kind of programs you will offer at your school. Based on information in the chart, you feel that the school should offer several courses in technical English.

There is a growing need to provide more technical English courses to international students. _____

_____

_____

_____

_____

_____

_____

_____

Revising

A. Read over your paragraph and look for ways to improve it. Use the Revising Checklist on page 66 to help you.

B. Check for errors in grammar, spelling, and punctuation. Copy your revised paragraph on a separate piece of paper.

Writing Exercise 2

Prewriting

Study the graph. It shows the amount of time it takes a typical runner to run five miles (eight kilometers) during the first eight years.

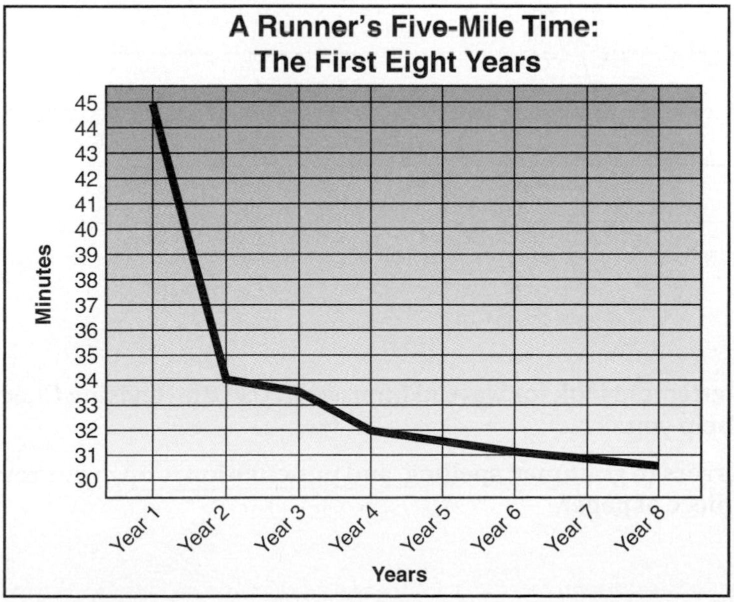

A Runner's Five-Mile Time: The First Eight Years

(Line graph: Y-axis labeled "Minutes" ranging from 30 to 45; X-axis labeled "Years" with Year 1 through Year 8. The line starts at 45 minutes in Year 1, drops to about 34 in Year 2, about 33.5 in Year 3, about 32 in Year 4, and gradually decreases to about 30.5 by Year 8.)

1. How long does it usually take to run five miles at the end of the first year? _____

2. When does the runner achieve the greatest decrease in the amount of time it takes to run five miles (eight kilometers)? _____

3. How long does it take a typical runner to run five miles (eight kilometers) at the end of the first year? _____

4. How long does it take at the end of the second year? _____

5. What happens during the following six years? _____

6. How long does it take during the seventh year? _____

7. By how many minutes does the time decrease during the first seven year period? _____

Writing

Read the situation. Complete the letter. Support the main idea with facts from the graph.

Situation: You are writing a letter to new members of your running club. Many of the new members are discouraged because it is taking them so long to run five miles. You want to encourage them to continue running.

Dear Members,

    I know that some of you are discouraged because it is taking you so long

to run five miles. But don't give up yet. _____

_____

_____

_____

_____

_____

_____

_____

_____

_____

Revising

A. **Read your letter and look for ways to improve it. Use the Revising Checklist on page 66 to help you.**

B. **Check for errors in grammar, spelling, and punctuation. Copy your revised letter on a separate piece of paper.**

USING QUOTES FOR SUPPORT

One of the strongest kinds of support is a quote from an expert on your topic. A quotation, or quote, is an exact reproduction of someone's spoken or written words. Put the quote right after the supporting sentence it relates to.

Read the paragraph and underline the quote.

Doctors and dieters agree that it is possible to lose weight by dieting, but the difficult part is keeping the weight off after you to lose it. Research indicates that although many people successfully lose weight by going on a diet, most people gain it back within three years. If you really want to lose weight permanently, diets alone are not enough. Exercise is very important too. According to Dr. Ian Field, "The key to permanent weight loss is getting people to change their lifestyles. Each person needs to find the right combination of diet and exercise." It's all about taking in fewer calories by eating less and burning off calories by exercising more.

GRAMMAR GUIDE: PUNCTUATING QUOTES

Be sure to punctuate quotes correctly. Read the rules for punctuating quotes.

RULES FOR PUNCTUATING QUOTES

- Put the person's exact words inside quotation marks.
- Use a comma after the words that introduce the quote.
- Capitalize the first word of the quote.
- Place periods, commas, and question marks inside the final quotation mark.

Introducing Quotes

It is important to let your reader know that a quotation is going to follow. Here are some examples of ways to introduce a quote into your paragraph.

- Dr. Elrich states, "Research shows that children who eat a healthy breakfast perform better at school."
- According to Dr. Elrich, "Research shows that children who eat a healthy breakfast perform better at school."

Study the list of common verbs used to introduce quotes.

VERBS THAT INTRODUCE QUOTES

claims	explains	observes	says	writes
comments	notes	points out	states	

Activity 1

Correct the errors in capitalization and punctuation in each sentence.

1. Mr. Whitnall explains it takes adults much longer than children to learn a new language

2. dr. jones claims sixty percent of my patients lost weight on this diet

3. Economist Marianne Watkins notes Americans spend more than $115 billion each year on fuel and electricity for their homes

4. According to Stephen Schneider even a small reduction of solar energy can affect agriculture worldwide

5. Amelia Earhart said adventure is worthwhile in itself

Activity 2

Work with a partner. Read each paragraph and the quote that follows. Decide where you think the quote should be inserted in the paragraph. Rewrite the paragraph on the lines provided.

1. High fuel prices and concern for the environment are causing many people to conserve energy. Some people are trying to save energy at home. For example, they are turning off lights and electrical appliances when they are not using them. They are also being careful about the amount of heat and air-conditioning they use. In addition, concerned people are conserving energy on the road. For instance, they are buying smaller, more fuel-efficient cars. Others are using public transportation or carpooling to save gas. Conserving energy at home and on the road are good ways to help the planet and save money.

"Set your thermostats at 75 degrees in the summer and 68 degrees in the winter to be comfortable and still save money and energy."
(Gerald Christopher, Director of the Energy Conservation Center)

_____

_____

_____

_____

_____

_____

_____

_____

_____

_____

_____

2.   Talking on a cell phone and driving do not mix. Unfortunately, too many people are combining the two activities, causing accidents that result in serious injury and death. In fact, research shows that people who use cell phones while driving are four times as likely to get into accidents that are serious enough to cause injury. Why? Using a cell phone is a big distraction. A survey of 1,200 drivers found that 73 percent talk on cell phones while driving. Cell phone use was highest among young, inexperienced drivers. It is no surprise that there has been a significant increase in the number of accidents caused by young people who were distracted while talking or texting on cell phones. These drivers were not paying attention to the road. Using cell phones while driving takes their eyes and ears off the road, and they can't give their full attention to driving.

"Drivers should have both hands on the wheel and their attention focused on the road, not on a cell phone conversation. I see more and more patients every week who are in the hospital because of cell phones!"
(Dr. Joel Weiss, emergency room doctor)

_____

_____

_____

_____

_____

_____

_____

_____

_____

_____

_____

_____

3.   Scientists around the world are studying animal behavior in a new way by using robo-animals. Robo-animals are robots that look, smell, and act like real animals. This new technology gives scientists a better opportunity to study living things in their natural environments rather than in labs. For example, researchers in Brussels created a robotic cockroach to observe how cockroaches move around in darkness. Students and professors at the University of Amherst in Massachusetts are using a robo-squirrel to learn about the survival instincts of squirrels. Scientists in Indiana have created a robotic lizard that helps them study the mating rituals of lizards. Robo-animals are giving scientists a unique way to learn more about how animals work in groups, court, avoid danger, and communicate with each other.

"We design the robo-animals carefully so they can pass in the wild. We pay special attention to the way the robo-animals smell, move, and sound. After all, a robot's ability to blend into its natural environment is the main reason we are using them." (Marlene Standish, engineer)

_____

_____

_____

_____

_____

_____

_____

_____

_____

_____

_____

_____

_____

_____

_____

PARAGRAPH POINTER: Providing Support

Remember that supporting sentences provide concrete evidence to convince readers that the main idea stated in the topic sentence is true. To find supporting evidence, ask yourself: What specific details can I use to show that what I wrote in my topic sentence is true? Supporting evidence often includes reasons, examples, personal anecdotes, facts, and statistics. Choose the type of support that best proves your main point.

YOU BE THE EDITOR

Read the paragraph. It contains seven mistakes. Correct the mistakes. Copy the corrected paragraph on a separate piece of paper.

Skyscrapers are on the rise. A new building called Burj Dubai in the United Arab Emirates city of dubai is being built and will be about 2,684 feets tall. That will make it the taller building in the world. Until recently, the world's tallest building was in Taipei, Taiwan. this towering office building in the heart of the busy capital city boasts 101 floors, which is where it gets it's name, Taipei 101. Recently, however, engineers and architects in Saudi Arabia announced plans to build a skyscraper that will surpass both Taipei 101 and Burj Dubai in high. The Mile-High Tower, as it is being called, will be twice as tall as the Burj Dubai. With so many tall buildings all over the world, tourists will have to get use to looking up more often.

ON YOUR OWN

Complete the following activities.

1. Find a chart or graph that interests you in a newspaper, magazine, or on the Internet and bring it to class. Write a paragraph explaining the information in the chart or graph. Share your chart and paragraph with your classmates.
2. Use the Internet or a library to find unusual facts about an animal from your country. Write a paragraph based on the facts.

EXPLAINING A PROCESS

When you explain how to do or make something, such as how to program your cell phone or how to make rice and beans, you are explaining a process. Similarly, when you explain how something works or happens, such as how an engine works or how your body digests food, you are also describing a process. When you describe a process, you should organize the steps according to time order.

Read the paragraph and underline the topic sentence. Then answer the questions.

One of the easiest ways to send out invitations to a party is to use a website called Evite. First, go to www.evite.com and click on *create an invitation*. Then, choose an invitation from one of the hundreds they offer. After that, type in the details of your party such as the date, address, and start time. Next, enter all the e-mail addresses of the people you want to invite. Finally, check over the invitation and click *send*. You won't believe how easy it is and Evite automatically keeps a record of who is coming to your party. I recommend that you try Evite the next time you are giving a party.

1. What steps does the author give?

   a. _____

   b. _____

   c. _____

   d. _____

   e. _____

2. How are the steps organized? _____

WRITING TOPIC SENTENCES FOR PROCESS PARAGRAPHS

The topic sentence of a process paragraph must identify the process and tell something about it. Write a topic sentence for the following paragraphs.

1. _____ First, get a copy of the receipt that shows you paid your tuition. Then take the receipt to the Student Affairs building. Go to the ID office and show the secretary your receipt. After that, get your picture taken. Remember to smile! Wait three minutes for your picture to be processed and your ID to be printed. Finally, sign your ID card and put it in your wallet.

2. _____ First of all, write your name and address in the upper left-hand corner of the envelope. Then write the name and address of the person you are mailing the letter to in the center of the envelope. This usually takes three lines. Put the name on the first line. Write the street address on the second line and the city and state on the third line. Remember to include the zip code. Finally, put a stamp in the upper right-hand corner. The most important thing to remember is to write neatly!

3. _____ First, fill a clean vase with water. Second, cut most of the flowers and greens so they are approximately two times the height of your vase. Then, cut a couple of the flowers two inches longer. After you are finished cutting the flowers, you can begin to put the greens in the vase. Now add the other flowers. Start at the outer edge of your vase. Put the longest flowers in the center of your arrangement. Then take a few steps back and admire your bouquet.

4. _____ First, put all the items you want to take on your bed and organize everything into groups. For example, put all your shoes in one group, all your clothes in another, all your underwear in a third, and so on. After that, place your shoes on the bottom of the suitcase. Then take your pants, fold them in half, roll them up, and place them in the bottom of the suitcase around the shoes. You can fill empty space on the bottom with socks and underwear. Next, fold and put flat items such as shirts and sweaters as a second layer. Finally, place your last layer of items in the suitcase. This way of packing helps you get organized and stay organized when you travel.

SIGNAL WORDS

PARAGRAPH POINTER: Time Order Signal Words

When you describe a process you put the steps in time order. In order to make the steps clear, you should use time order signal words to guide the reader from one step to the next. Review the signal words on page 30.

Complete the following paragraph using signal words.

It is very easy to make good popcorn. __First__, put three or four tablespoons of oil in a large heavy pot. _____, heat the oil on a high flame until one kernel of popcorn pops when you drop it into the hot oil. When the oil is hot enough, pour one-quarter cup of popcorn into the pot and cover it with a lid. _____, reduce the flame to medium and begin to shake the pot gently. Continue shaking the pot until all the corn has popped. _____, empty the popcorn into a large bowl and add melted butter and salt.

GRAMMAR GUIDE: IMPERATIVE SENTENCES

When you explain how to do or make something, you often use imperative sentences. Imperative sentences are different from regular sentences because they do not have a subject. The implied subject is *you*. Imperative sentences are used to give advice or instructions, or to express a request or a command.

A. **Study the sentences in the chart. Notice that each one begins with the base form of a verb. For negative imperative forms use: *Do* + *not* (don't) + base form of the verb.**

AFFIRMATIVE SENTENCES	**Fold** the paper in half.
	Complete the application.
NEGATIVE SENTENCE	**Do not take** this medicine during the day.

B. **What would you tell someone who is going to drive a car for the first time in your country? Write four imperative sentences.**

1. _Follow the speed limit._
2. _____
3. _____
4. _____

C. **What would you tell someone going on a job interview? Write four imperative sentences.**

1. _____
2. _____
3. _____
4. _____

WRITING PROCESS PARAGRAPHS

Activity 1

A. The following sentences describe how to make a chocolate sundae, but they are not in the correct time order. Find the topic sentence and put a *1* in front of it. Use the signal words to help you put the steps in the right order, from *2* to *5*.

Making a Sundae

_____ Next, cover the fudge with whipped cream.

_____ Chocolate sundaes are one of the easiest desserts to make.

_____ Finally, sprinkle chopped nuts on the whipped cream and put a cherry on top.

_____ Then pour two tablespoons of hot fudge sauce over the ice cream.

_____ First, put two or three large scoops of your favorite kind of ice cream in a dish.

B. Use the steps to write a paragraph.

_____

_____

_____

_____

_____

_____

_____

Activity 2

A. The following sentences describe what to do if someone is choking. First, find the topic sentence. Then number the sentences in the right order.

The Heimlich Maneuver

_____ Then make a fist with one hand and grasp the fist with your other hand. Put your hands just below the person's rib cage.

_____ The Heimlich maneuver is a method that anyone can use to help someone who is choking on a piece of food.

_____ Finally, press your fist into the victim's abdomen with a quick upward movement.

_____ The first thing you should do is stand behind the choking person and put your arms around the person's waist.

_____ If the person is still choking, you may need to repeat the maneuver.

_____

_____

_____

_____

_____

_____

_____

_____

_____

Activity 3

A. **Study the pictures. They show how to pot a plant. Use the pictures to number the steps in the correct time order.**

Potting a Plant

_____ Make a hole in center of soil.

_____ Press soil down with thumbs.

__1__ Cover bottom of pot with small stones.

_____ Drop plant into soil.

_____ Put two inches of soil on top of rocks.

_____ Water plant.

_____ Add soil until it almost reaches top of pot.

B. Use the steps to complete the paragraph.

It is easy to pot a plant if you follow the right procedure. _____

_____

_____

_____

_____

_____

_____

_____

Writing Exercise

Prewriting

A. Choose one of the following processes to write about.

How to:

- plan a party
- make your favorite dish
- change a flat tire
- get cash from an automatic teller machine

- study for an exam
- program your cell phone
- plant a garden
- send or receive an e-mail

B. Make a list of all the steps in the process.

_____ _____

_____ _____

_____ _____

_____ _____

_____ _____

_____ _____

C. Number the steps so they are in the correct time order.

D. Write a topic sentence that identifies the process and tells something about it.

_____

Writing

Write the first draft of a paragraph describing the process. Begin with your topic sentence. Use the list of steps from your prewriting as a guide.

_____

_____

_____

_____

_____

_____

_____

_____

Revising

A. **Read over your paragraph and look for ways to improve it. Use the Revising Checklist on page 66 to help you. As you revise your paragraph, think about these questions.**

1. Are your steps in correct time order?

2. Did you leave out any important steps in the process?

3. Did you use imperative sentences?

B. **Check for errors in grammar, spelling, and punctuation. Copy your revised paragraph on a separate piece of paper.**

DESCRIBING STEPS IN AN EXPERIMENT

Describing processes is very important in scientific and technical fields.

A. **Study the following lab report.**

WATER EXPANSION EXPERIMENT

Purpose: To show that water expands when frozen

Materials: A glass jar, water

Procedure:
1. Fill the glass jar halfway with water.
2. Mark the outside of the jar at water level.
3. Put the jar in the freezer until the water freezes.
4. Observe and mark the new water level.

Results: The level of the frozen water is higher.

B. **Read the paragraph that describes the experiment and answer the questions.**

You can do a simple experiment to prove that water expands when it is frozen. All you need is an empty glass jar. First, fill half the jar with water. Then mark the water level on the outside of the jar. After that, put the jar in a freezer until the water freezes. When the water is frozen, take the jar out of the freezer and observe the new water level. You will see that the level of the frozen water is higher. This proves that water expands when it is frozen.

1. What is the topic sentence? _____

_____

2. What signal words are used in the paragraph? _____

_____

3. How many steps are described? _____

Writing Exercise 1

Prewriting

Read the following lab report. Discuss it with a classmate.

SOLAR ENERGY EXPERIMENT

<u>Purpose</u>: To show that black is a better collector of solar energy than white

<u>Materials</u>: 2 tin cans, black and white paint, room thermometer

<u>Procedure</u>:
1. Paint the cans—one black, one white.
2. Fill the cans with water.
3. Put the cans in direct sunlight for three hours.
4. Check the temperature of the water in the cans and compare.

<u>Results</u>: The temperature of the water in the black can is higher.

Writing

Now use the information to write a paragraph describing the process of the experiment. Remember to begin with a topic sentence and use signal words.

_____

_____

_____

_____

_____

_____

_____

Revising

A. Read over your paragraph and look for ways to improve it. Use the Revising Checklist on page 66 to help you.

B. Check for errors in grammar, spelling, and punctuation. Copy your revised paragraph on a separate piece of paper.

Writing Exercise 2

Prewriting

A. Study the diagram. It shows the four stages in the life cycle of a butterfly: eggs, caterpillar, chrysalis, and adult butterfly.

Life Cycle of a Butterfly

1.

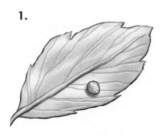

A butterfly lays **eggs** on plant leaves and stems.

2.

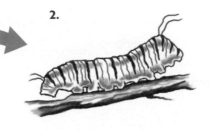

Five days later, a small **caterpillar** hatches from each egg. For a few weeks the **caterpillar** spends most of its time eating leaves and growing bigger.

4.

The adult **butterfly** emerges from the chrysalis and looks for another **butterfly** to mate with. After mating, the female **butterfly** lays her eggs and the whole cycle begins again. Adult butterflies usually live for only two weeks!

3.

The caterpillar stops eating and growing. It sheds its skin and becomes a pupa. The pupa stays inside a hard shell called a **chrysalis** for several weeks. Inside the **chrysalis**, the pupa changes from a caterpillar's body to a butterfly's body.

B. Discuss the four stages in the life cycle with a partner. What happens in each stage? How long does each stage last?

Writing

Use the information from the diagram to write the first draft of a paragraph about the life cycle of a butterfly. Remember to begin with a topic sentence and use signal words.

_____

_____

_____

_____

_____

_____

_____

_____

_____

_____

_____

Revising

A. Read over your paragraph and look for ways to improve it. Use the Revising Checklist on page 66 to help you.

B. Check for errors in grammar, spelling, and punctuation. Copy your revised paragraph on a separate piece of paper.

GIVING DIRECTIONS

When you explain to someone how to get from one place to another place, you are giving directions. In order to make your directions clear, you need to use words that signal both time order and space order.

A. Study this list of useful words for writing directions.

DIRECTION SIGNAL WORDS	
Continue _____	across the street from _____
Go as far as _____	between _____ and _____
Go north (or south, east, west)	in the middle of the _____
Go one block (or two blocks, etc.)	next door to
Go past _____	on the corner
Go straight (until you come to _____)	on the left (or the right)
Turn left (or right)	on the left side (or the right side)

B. Look carefully at the map of the historical area of Philadelphia. Find the Visitor Center on the map. Where is it located?

C. Read the directions.

In order to get from the Visitor Center to the U.S. Mint, follow these directions. First, go north two blocks from the Visitor Center. Then turn left on Arch Street. Continue two blocks on Arch Street to Fifth Street. The U.S. Mint is on your right.

D. Situation: You work at the Visitor Center. Write directions from the Visitor Center to each of the following places for a tour guidebook.

1. Liberty Bell Pavillion

   _____

   _____

   _____

   _____

   _____

2. Free Quaker Meeting House

   _____

   _____

   _____

   _____

   _____

3. First Bank of the United States

_____

_____

_____

_____

4. Franklin Court

_____

_____

_____

_____

5. Graff House

_____

_____

_____

_____

YOU BE THE EDITOR

Read the paragraph. It contains nine mistakes. Correct the mistakes. Copy the corrected paragraph on a separate piece of paper.

It is not difficult to remove the shell from a lobster if you follow these step. First, you should to put the lobster on it's back and remove the two large claws and tail section. After that, You must also twist off the flippers at end of tail section. After these are twisted off, use you fingers to push the lobster meat out of the tail in one piece. Next, remove the black vein. From the tail meat. Finally, before you sit down to enjoy your meal, break open the claws with a nutcracker and remove the meat.

ON YOUR OWN

Choose one of the following activities to complete.

1. Draw a simple map of your neighborhood. Label the streets and important buildings. Practice the vocabulary of giving directions by writing directions from your house to several other places. Check your directions by having another student follow them.

2. Write a paragraph that tells how to protect yourself when a hurricane, blizzard, tornado, or other natural disaster is forecast for your area.

3. Write a paragraph that describes the steps involved in getting a driver's license.

WRITING DESCRIPTIONS

Writing a description is like creating a picture using words. The key to writing a good description is using specific details that create exactly the picture you want. In this chapter you will learn how to write descriptions of people, places, and things.

DESCRIBING PEOPLE

When you describe a person, you explain what he or she looks and acts like. You write about physical characteristics such as height, weight, and hair color. You can also write about the person's style of clothing and way of talking and walking. The key to writing a good description is to use details that help the reader imagine the person you are describing.

Read the paragraph and underline the descriptive details.

> The police are searching for a stylish woman who cleverly stole a diamond ring from Dayton's Jewelry Store. According to the store manager, the woman has short, curly brown hair and big blue eyes. She is average height, slender, and about sixty-five years old. When she was last seen, she was elegantly dressed in a grey hat, a black and white plaid coat, black pants, and black high-heeled boots. She speaks softly and uses her hands a lot when she talks. She doesn't look like someone who would steal a ring!

Activity

A. Read this telephone conversation.

Lucia: Hi Clara. I have a big problem and I hope you can help me.

Clara: What's the problem? I'll help if I can.

Lucia: My cousin is coming home tonight from his trip to Europe and I'm supposed to pick him up at the airport at seven o'clock. The problem is that I just found out I have to work late tonight. Can you possibly pick him up for me?

Clara: Sure. What airline is he taking?

Lucia: British Airways. Flight 179.

Clara: OK. But how will I recognize him?

Lucia: Well, he's medium height and average weight.

Clara: That could be almost anyone. Can you be more specific?

Lucia: Well, his hair is blond and curly. He wears glasses. I almost forgot! He has a beard.

Clara: What's his name?

Lucia: Ernie Norton.

Clara: OK, no problem. I'll find him.

Lucia: Great. Thank you so much!

At the last minute, Clara is unable to go to the airport. Her brother Ben has agreed to pick up Ernie instead. Clara is writing a note to Ben describing Ernie so that he will be able to find him. What should Clara's note say? The following questions will help you.

- Is he tall or short?
- Is he fat or thin?
- What color hair does he have?
- Is his hair curly or straight?
- Does he wear glasses?
- Is there anything about him that you notice immediately?

B. Pretend you are Clara. Write a note to Ben describing Ernie.

> Dear Ben,
>
> _____
>
> _____
>
> _____
>
> _____
>
> _____

TOPIC SENTENCES FOR DESCRIPTIVE PARAGRAPHS

The topic sentence of a descriptive paragraph should include who or what you are describing and your dominant impression of the person, place, or thing.

Read the following sample topic sentences and discuss the questions with a partner.

1. My grandfather is getting old, but he is still handsome and careful about his appearance.
    a. Who is the author describing?
    b. How does the author feel about the subject?

2. Although it was made with love, the sweater my aunt gave me is one of the ugliest things I've ever seen.
    a. What is the author describing?
    b. How does the author feel about the object?

3. My most treasured possession is the beautiful pearl ring my grandmother gave me.
    a. What is the author describing?
    b. How does the author feel about the object?

4. My brother's new girlfriend is absolutely gorgeous.
    a. Who is the author describing?
    b. How does the author feel about her?

5. The first time I met Jason, I thought he appeared frail and sickly.
    a. Who is the author describing?
    b. How does the author feel about him?

6. My favorite piece of furniture is an old leather armchair that has been in our family room for many years.
    a. What is the author describing?
    b. How does the author feel about the object?

7. Our new teacher is tall and thin and she looks very stern.
    a. Who is the author describing?
    b. How does the author feel about her?

8. I can't wait to get rid of our old, rusty lawn mower.
    a. What is the author describing?
    b. How does the author feel about the object?

Descriptive Words

When you describe what a person looks like, you write about physical characteristics such as height, weight, and hair color. Here are some words that can help you.

WORDS FOR DESCRIBING PEOPLE				
Height	**Age**	**Body Type**	**Hair**	**Features**
medium	ancient	athletic	blond	beard
short	elderly	frail	curly	dimple
shortish	middle-aged	heavy	dark	freckles
tall	old	muscular	light	glasses
tallish	teenaged	petite	long	mole
	young	plump	red	mustache
		skinny	short	scar
		stocky	straight	wrinkles
		thin	wavy	

Writing Exercise 1

Prewriting

A. Choose someone you know well to describe. For example, a friend, relative, classmate, teacher, or coworker. Make a list of descriptive details about the person.

_____   _____

_____   _____

_____   _____

B. Look over your list. What is your main impression about the person? Use your main impression to write a topic sentence.

_____

Writing

Write the first draft of a description of the person.

_____

_____

_____

_____

_____

_____

_____

_____

Revising

A. Read over your description and make sure your descriptive details support your topic sentence. You can also use the Revising Checklist on page 66 to help you.

B. Check for errors in grammar, spelling, and punctuation. Copy your revised description on a separate piece of paper.

Writing Exercise 2

A. Choose someone in your class to describe.

B. Write a short description of that person, but do not mention his or her name. Remember to include details about height, hair color, distinguishing features, and so on. Write your description on a separate piece of paper.

C. Give the description to your teacher. The teacher will give you another classmate's description. Read the description you were given. Can you guess who it describes?

Writing Exercise 3

Pretend you are one of the *paparazzi*—photographers who follow famous people and take their pictures. You have just taken a good photo of a famous person and you contact a magazine to try to sell your photo. Name the person and describe the photograph. What does he or she look like in the picture? What is he or she wearing? What other things or people are in the picture? If you cannot imagine a photo, look for one in a magazine or newspaper and describe it.

Example:

I have a photograph of Prince William. He is walking on a London street. He is wearing sunglasses and a gray raincoat. He has a new hairstyle, and he is holding hands with a beautiful lady. She looks much older than the prince! They are both carrying small shopping bags with the name of a famous jeweler on them.

DESCRIBING THINGS

Read the paragraph and answer the questions that follow.

> I bought a beautiful antique gold watch to give my father for his birthday. Although it's more than sixty years old, it's in excellent condition. The round face of the watch is white with shiny raised gold numbers and thin black hands. It's about 36 millimeters in diameter. The back of the watch has a small scratch and the letters *JLH* engraved on it. They are probably the original owner's initials. The band is made of soft brown leather with a gold buckle. I know my father will love the watch because it stills keeps perfect time after all these years.

1. What is the author describing?

   _____

2. How does the author feel about the object?

   _____

3. What details does the author use to describe the pocket watch?

   _____   _____

   _____   _____

   _____   _____

4. What is the concluding sentence?

   _____

   _____

Descriptive Details

The supporting sentences in a descriptive paragraph should include details that create a picture with words. They often include information about size, weight, shape, pattern or decoration, color, material, and any special features.

PARAGRAPH POINTER: Sensory Words

When you write a description, you can use words that relate to the senses of sight, sound, touch, smell, and taste. These are called sensory words. Sensory words help the reader imagine what you are describing.

Here are some common sensory words you can use to describe objects.

COMMON SENSORY WORDS

Color	Shape	Size	Smell	Taste	Texture
black	flat	average	fresh	bitter	rough
blue	oval	big	fruity	bland	sharp
orange	rectangular	enormous	mild	fruity	silky
purple	round	huge	pungent	nutty	smooth
yellow	square	small	smoky	oily	soft
	triangular	tiny	strong	rich	
				salty	
				sour	
				spicy	
				sweet	

Write a few sentences to describe each of the following things. Use sensory words in your descriptions.

1   your favorite food

_____

_____

_____

2.   a food you dislike

_____

_____

_____

3.   your favorite toy when you were a child

_____

_____

_____

4.   your favorite item of clothing

_____

_____

_____

GRAMMAR GUIDE: ORDER OF ADJECTIVES

When you use more than one adjective in a series to describe something, they usually follow a certain order. The chart shows the typical order of adjectives in English. However, there are many exceptions and the rules are complicated. Over time, as you learn more English, the order of adjectives will become more natural.

A. Study the chart.

	OPINION	SIZE	AGE	SHAPE	COLOR	ORIGIN	MATERIAL	PURPOSE	NOUN
a, an, the	soft		new			Egyptian	cotton	hand	towel
	ugly		old		blue			winter	sweater
		small		round			wooden	salad	bowl

B. Here are some examples from each category of adjectives. Add three adjectives for each group.

1. Opinion or judgment: beautiful, ugly, easy, fast, interesting, _____,

   _____, _____

2. Size: small, tall, huge, short, big, _____, _____,

   _____

3. Age: young, old, antique, new, historic, ancient, _____,

   _____, _____

4. Shape: round, flat, square, rectangular, _____, _____,

   _____

5. Color: red, black, green, purple, _____, _____,

   _____

6. Origin: Mexican, Asian, American, Japanese, _____,

   _____, _____

7. Material: wooden, metal, plastic, glass, paper, _____,

   _____, _____

8. Purpose: racing (car), baseball (cap), _____, _____,

   _____

C. Work in small groups and compare your adjectives.

D. Choose the correct order of adjectives to complete the sentence.

1. I invited a(n) _____ student to the meeting.
   a. young engineering intelligent
   b. intelligent young engineering
   c. engineering young intelligent

2. She wore a _____ dress to the party.
   a. lovely blue cotton
   b. cotton blue lovely
   c. blue lovely cotton

3. I found _____ coins in the drawer.
   a. silver three old
   b. old silver three
   c. three old silver

4. The restaurant serves _____ food.
   a. delicious gourmet French
   b. French delicious gourmet
   c. gourmet delicious French

5. There is a(n) _____ table in the corner of the room.
   a. square wooden old
   b. old square wooden
   c. old wooden square

6. I saw a(n) _____ movie last night.
   a. new Japanese exciting
   b. exciting new Japanese
   c. Japanese new exciting

7. The clown wore a _____ hat.
   a. big red plastic
   b. red big plastic
   c. plastic big red

Describing Items

You have a small e-commerce business that sells travel goods. This month you are featuring a 30-percent-off coupon for new customers on five of your best-selling products. Read the product descriptions for the first three items. Then write descriptions for the other two on page 119.

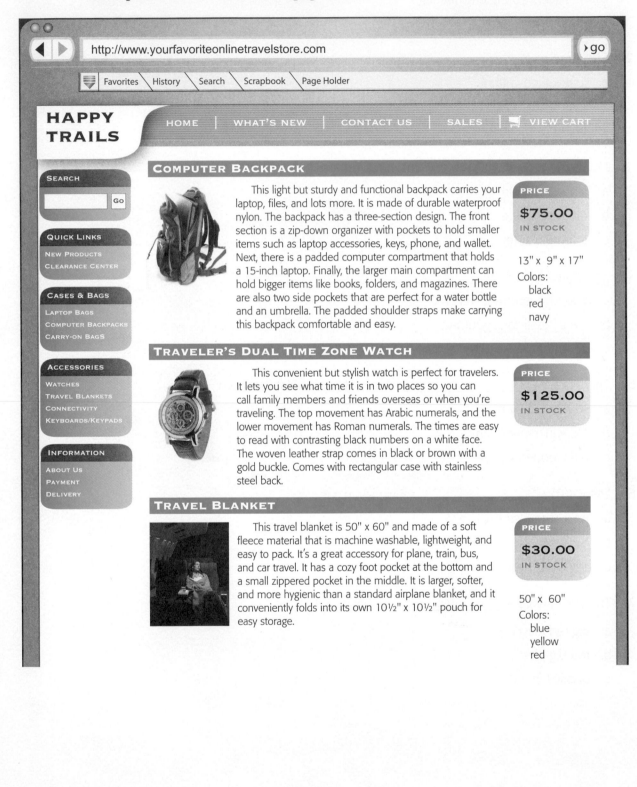

http://www.yourfavoriteonlinetravelstore.com ▸go

Favorites | History | Search | Scrapbook | Page Holder

HAPPY TRAILS

HOME | WHAT'S NEW | CONTACT US | SALES | 🛒 VIEW CART

SEARCH
[ ] Go

QUICK LINKS
NEW PRODUCTS
CLEARANCE CENTER

CASES & BAGS
LAPTOP BAGS
COMPUTER BACKPACKS
CARRY-ON BAGS

ACCESSORIES
WATCHES
TRAVEL BLANKETS
CONNECTIVITY
KEYBOARDS/KEYPADS

INFORMATION
ABOUT US
PAYMENT
DELIVERY

COMPUTER BACKPACK

This light but sturdy and functional backpack carries your laptop, files, and lots more. It is made of durable waterproof nylon. The backpack has a three-section design. The front section is a zip-down organizer with pockets to hold smaller items such as laptop accessories, keys, phone, and wallet. Next, there is a padded computer compartment that holds a 15-inch laptop. Finally, the larger main compartment can hold bigger items like books, folders, and magazines. There are also two side pockets that are perfect for a water bottle and an umbrella. The padded shoulder straps make carrying this backpack comfortable and easy.

PRICE
$75.00
IN STOCK

13" x 9" x 17"
Colors:
  black
  red
  navy

TRAVELER'S DUAL TIME ZONE WATCH

This convenient but stylish watch is perfect for travelers. It lets you see what time it is in two places so you can call family members and friends overseas or when you're traveling. The top movement has Arabic numerals, and the lower movement has Roman numerals. The times are easy to read with contrasting black numbers on a white face. The woven leather strap comes in black or brown with a gold buckle. Comes with rectangular case with stainless steel back.

PRICE
$125.00
IN STOCK

TRAVEL BLANKET

This travel blanket is 50" x 60" and made of a soft fleece material that is machine washable, lightweight, and easy to pack. It's a great accessory for plane, train, bus, and car travel. It has a cozy foot pocket at the bottom and a small zippered pocket in the middle. It is larger, softer, and more hygienic than a standard airplane blanket, and it conveniently folds into its own 10½" x 10½" pouch for easy storage.

PRICE
$30.00
IN STOCK

50" x 60"
Colors:
  blue
  yellow
  red

CARRY-ON BAG

PRICE

$ _____

IN STOCK

_____

_____

_____

_____

_____

_____

_____

_____

_____

TRAVEL WALLET

PRICE

$ _____

IN STOCK

_____

_____

_____

_____

_____

_____

_____

_____

_____

Writing Exercise 1

Prewriting

A. Pretend that you have lost something that is special to you. Draw a picture of it and describe the object to a friend.

B. Make a list of descriptive details about the object. Answer these questions to help you make your list:

- What size is it?
- What shape is it?
- What color is it?

- How heavy is it?
- What are its main characteristics?
- What other thing does it look like?

_____

_____

_____

_____

_____

_____

C. Write a topic sentence for your description that includes the object and how you feel about it.

_____

Writing

A. Write a description of the object so other people can help you find it. Use the list of descriptive details from your prewriting as a guide.

_____

_____

_____

_____

_____

_____

_____

_____

_____

_____

_____

_____

B. Give your description to a classmate and ask him or her to draw the object using your description.

Revising

Compare the picture to the description. How are they alike? What are the differences? The differences should give you clues to help you revise your paragraph. After you revise your paragraph, copy the final draft on a separate piece of paper.

Writing Exercise 2

Prewriting

A. You are going to write a description of something you want to sell online. Before you write a description, read the sample below of a game table for sale on an auction website.

For sale:

This beautiful oak game table is a great addition to any room. It is 32 inches in height with four sturdy legs. The top is a 28-inch square with a reversible inset game board. One side is for chess or checkers, and the other side is for backgammon. There is a handy felt-lined drawer for storing all your game pieces. You will have years of fun with this game table.

B. Decide what you want to write a description about. Draw or take a picture of it. Then make a list of descriptive details about the object.

_____   _____

_____   _____

_____   _____

C. Write a topic sentence for your description that includes the object and something special about it.

_____

Writing

Write a description of the object you want to sell. Use the list of descriptive details from your prewriting as a guide.

_____

_____

_____

_____

Revising

A. Read over your description and make sure the details support your topic sentence. Add any other details to improve your description.

B. Check for errors in grammar, spelling, and punctuation. Copy your revised description on a separate piece of paper.

Writing Exercise 3

A. Look around your classroom. Choose something in the room to describe.

B. Write a short description of that thing, but do not mention what it is. Remember to include details about size, shape, color, texture, and so on.

C. Exchange descriptions with a classmate. Read your classmate's description. Can you guess what it is?

DESCRIBING PLACES

In Chapter 5, you learned that when you describe a place, you use spatial order to organize the details according to their location. Choose a logical method to follow that suits the place you are describing such as left to right, top to bottom, or front to back.

A. **Read the postcard.**

Hi,

    I'm sorry I didn't get to see you while you were in Boston. It was so hot here that we went to our favorite campsite in the mountains. It's near the top of Mount Greylock in the Berkshires. The view is spectacular in the evening. The sky turns bright orange and pink as the sun sets behind the hills in the distance. From the tower at the top of the mountain you can look down at the valleys and rivers below. The hiking trails are long and shady. There's a small pond near the campsite where we can swim when we get hot. The site is very clean and rarely crowded. Best of all, there's always a refreshing cool breeze! Let me know when you'll be in Boston again.

Love,
Carolyn

Sharon Laroche
84 Maple Street
Hawthorne, NY 10532

B. **What details does Carolyn use to describe Mount Greylock?**

_____   _____

_____   _____

_____   _____

Descriptive Words

Using descriptive language is also important when you describe places.

Study the chart.

DESCRIPTIVE WORDS FOR PLACES		
clean	hot	quiet
cold	humid	rural
colorful	industrial	sandy
cool	modern	smoky
crowded	mountainous	spectacular
flat	narrow	wide
fresh	old	windy
hilly		

Activity

Look at the picture. Pretend you are on vacation there and write a postcard to a friend describing the place. Use at least five descriptive words from the list. Underline the descriptive words you use.

Writing Exercise 1

Prewriting

A. In this activity you will write a description of the hometown of one of your classmates. If everyone is from the same place, ask your partner questions about another city he or she has visited. Talk to your partner about his or her hometown. Use the suggestions below to make a list of questions to ask your partner.

1. What is the name of your hometown and where is it located?
2. How big is it?
3. What are the main geographical features?
4. Are there any interesting stories or historical facts associated with your hometown?
5. What interesting places are to the north, south, east, or west of your hometown?
6. Does your hometown have a college or university?
7. Does your hometown have a shopping mall?
8. What is the most impressive thing about your hometown?
9. What are some interesting things to do and see there?
10. What are the people like?
11. What is the weather like?

B. Ask your partner the questions about his or her hometown and take notes.

Writing

Use the information you have about your partner's hometown to write the first draft of the paragraph. Be sure to give the name of the place and say something special about it in the topic sentence.

_____

_____

_____

_____

_____

_____

_____

_____

_____

Revising

A. Now ask your partner to read your paragraph. Does he or she have any suggestions? Revise your paragraph based on your partner's suggestions. You can also use the Revising Checklist on page 66 to help you.

B. Check for errors in grammar, spelling, and punctuation. Copy your revised paragraph on a separate piece of paper.

Writing Exercise 2

Prewriting

A. **Chose one of the following topics to write about.**
- your favorite place to go and relax such as a beach, a park, or your bedroom
- your favorite place to eat such as your grandmother's kitchen or a restaurant you like
- your favorite place to go with your friends such as a mall or a coffee shop

B. **Make a list of details describing the place.**

_____   _____

_____   _____

_____   _____

C. **Write a topic sentence that names the place and gives your main impression of it.**

_____

D. **Cross out details that do not support the topic sentence.**

E. **Choose a pattern of spatial organization such as left to right or far to near.**

Writing

Use your topic sentence and details from your list to write the first draft of
the paragraph.

_____

_____

_____

_____

_____

_____

_____

Revising

A. **Read over your description. Use the Revising Checklist on page 66 to help you revise
your paragraph. Also, think about these questions as you revise your paragraph.**

1. Did you include enough specific details about the place?

2. What other details can you add to make your description clearer?

3. Did you use spatial order to organize the supporting sentences?

B. **Check for errors in grammar, spelling, and punctuation. Copy your revised
paragraph on a separate piece of paper.**

YOU BE THE EDITOR

Read the paragraph. It contains seven mistakes. Correct the mistakes. Copy the corrected paragraph on a separate piece of paper.

Dog Missing

My adorable dog, Bette, is missing. She is a small black poodle with browns eyes. her hair is short and curly. Bette weighs 8 pounds and is about one and a half foots long. She has a short tail, long, floppy ears, and small feet. She is wear a silver collar with an ID tag on it. She is very friendly around people and love children. I have had Bette for six years, since she was a puppy. I missing her very much. I am offering a $50 reward for anyone which finds Bette. Please call me at 305-892-7671.

ON YOUR OWN

Choose one of the following activities to complete.

1. Write a description of one of the people in this picture.

2. Write a description of your favorite movie star, musician, or athlete.
3. If you could invent something new, what product would you invent? Describe your invention using specific details.
4. Describe a well-known building in your hometown.

EXPRESSING YOUR OPINION

When you write, it is often necessary to express your opinion. Your goal is to persuade the reader that your opinion is correct. After you state your opinion, you need to give reasons, facts, or examples to support it.

"The roof leaks, the furnace doesn't work, and the plumbing needs repair...but it's located on the greatest planet in the universe!"

EXPRESSING OPINIONS

Read the article and the two opinion paragraphs. Answer the questions that follow.

The number of children in public schools in the United States who speak little or no English is increasing rapidly. For example, students in the Washington, D.C., school system speak more than 100 different languages and dialects. In the California public schools, one out of six students was born outside the United States, and one out of three speaks a language other than English at home. These students and their teachers face many challenges, including what language to use in the classroom. Some people believe that children who do not speak English should be taught in their native language. Others believe that these children should be taught in English only.

1.   In my opinion, children who do not speak English should be taught in their native language. First of all, these children will feel more comfortable in a strange school if they hear and speak their native language. If they spend most of the day unable to understand what teachers and other students are saying, they may feel lonely and

confused. In addition, they will be able to understand subjects like math, history, and science more easily if they are taught in their native language. This way they can concentrate on the new content information and not be distracted by decoding a new language at the same time. Finally, there is no research evidence proving that English-only programs are better or even appropriate for children who are still developing their basic cognitive-linguistic skills. For example, learning how to read for the first time is too complicated in a language that a student does not understand.

a. What is the author's opinion?

b. What three major reasons does the author give to support his or her opinion?

_____

_____

_____

2.   I believe that children of immigrants should be taught in English. First, they will learn the new language more quickly if all their subjects are taught in English. Students who spend the whole school day listening to English will learn more idioms, general vocabulary, and technical words. Second, children of immigrants will feel less isolated if they are taught in the same language as the rest of the children. They won't be pulled out of some classes and will be able to make friends more easily. Finally, they will be able to perform better on standardized tests if they have learned the material in their classes in English. They will be familiar with standard test instructions in English and will know what kinds of questions to expect.

a. What is the author's opinion?

b. What three major reasons does the author give to support his or her opinion?

_____

_____

_____

PARAGRAPH POINTER: Using Reasons

A good opinion paragraph should give the reader something to think about. It should include convincing reasons presented in a logical order.

Activity

Read the two opinion paragraphs about the Internet. Cross out the irrelevant sentence in each one.

1.   In my opinion, the Internet is the most valuable tool we have today for accessing information. No matter what or who you're looking for, you can probably find the information you need quickly and easily on the Internet. Information that used to be difficult or time-consuming to find is now just a few clicks away. For example, by using search engines on the Internet, it's easy to locate long lost friends or family members.

In addition, you can find scholarly information on almost any topic you want to study even if you don't have access to a university library. From literature and history, to medicine and music, the Internet has thousands of Web sites dedicated to providing information. This means that everyone has equal access to information. The word Internet was first used in 1982. Finally, the Internet allows new information to be transmitted almost instantly. As soon as something happens in the news, you can read about it on the Internet. In today's world, where the more you know the better off you are, the Internet may very well hold the key to success!

2.   I think there is too much information available on the Internet today. First of all, much of the information on the Internet is unreliable and misleading. With no one regulating or fact-checking what is put on the Internet, it is very hard to know if the information you're reading is even true. It's easy to find the definition of a word on the Internet. In addition, much of the information that is readily available on the Internet can be dangerous in the wrong hands. For instance, it is easy to gain access to other people's personal information. Pictures, names, addresses, and phone numbers are only a few clicks away. Even credit card numbers are easy for hackers to access. Finally, all of this information can lead to something called "information overload." If you don't know what information overload is, don't worry. There is a lot of information about it on the Internet! Basically, information overload happens when you have too much information to make a decision or remain informed about a topic. In conclusion, there is definitely far too much information on the Internet—some of which is personal, dangerous, or simply false.

TOPIC SENTENCES THAT EXPRESS AN OPINION

When your topic sentence is an opinion, you can begin the sentence with one of these phrases:

- I am against
- I support
- I am in favor of
- I think ('that')
- I believe (that)
- In my opinion,
- I oppose

Write a topic sentence for each paragraph.

1.   _____ First of all, more public transportation will help solve the traffic problem in our city. Secondly, public transportation provides an inexpensive means of transportation for people who cannot afford to buy cars. Most importantly, public transportation is better for the environment because it produces less air pollution.

2.   _____ The most obvious point is that you can earn extra money. Secondly, working part-time and going to school will help you learn to manage your time more effectively. Hopefully this will make you a more organized person. Finally, you can gain some work experience that will help you get a better job when you graduate.

3. _____ First of all, genetically modified (GM) plants can survive weed killers. That means they require less chemical spraying. Many GM plants even produce their own insecticides. Planting GM crops also lowers farmers' costs. Finally, when farmers plant GM crops, they increase their output. That means more food at a lower cost.

Writing Exercise

Prewriting

A. **Discuss the sentences with a partner. Decide which ones support the opinion that watching TV is good for children. Mark those with a G. Also decide which sentences support the opinion that watching TV has bad effects on children. Mark those with a B.**

_B_ 1. Watching TV is too passive.

_____ 2. Watching TV can be an educational experience.

_____ 3. There is too much violence on TV.

_____ 4. TV provides windows to different countries, cultures, and languages.

_____ 5. Children get a biased picture of society from TV.

_____ 6. TV gives children free entertainment and a time to relax quietly.

_____ 7. Children are too influenced by the commercials they see on TV.

B. **Fill in the outlines. The topic sentences are given. Use the sentences from Exercise A as main supporting points. You will fill in the details later.**

Outline 1

Topic Sentence: Watching TV is good for children.

Main Supporting Point 1: _Watching TV can be an educational experience._

Detail: _TV stations such as the Learning Channel, Animal Planet, Discovery, and the History Channel teach children about science, history, and the arts._

Main Supporting Point 2: _____

Detail: _____

_____

Main Supporting Point 3: _____

Detail: _____

_____

Outline 2

Topic Sentence: Watching TV has bad effects on children.

Main Supporting Point 1: _____

Detail: _____

_____

Main Supporting Point 2: _____

Detail: _____

_____

Main Supporting Point 3: _____

Detail: _____

_____

Main Supporting Point 4: _____

Detail: _____

_____

_____

C. **Now read and discuss the list of sentences that follow. They are details that go with the main supporting points. Complete the outlines in Exercise B by writing each detail under the appropriate major supporting points.**

- Television can provide a pleasant escape from the stress that many children experience.
- Many TV shows reinforce negative gender and racial stereotypes.
- TV shows on the Learning Channel, Animal Planet, Discovery, and the History Channel teach children about science, history, and the arts.
- Documentaries show children what is going in different parts of the world.
- A recent study shows that children in the United States see 40,000 commercials each year.
- There are more than seven acts of violence per hour on prime-time TV, and many violent TV shows are on Saturday mornings, when children are watching.
- Instead of sitting in front of the TV, children should be engaging in more creative behaviors and doing more active activities outdoors.
- Some of the most violent TV shows are cartoons, where violence is portrayed as funny, and the realistic effects of violence are not shown.
- Long-time favorites such as *Sesame Street* and *Mr. Rogers* can help develop children's socialization and learning skills.
- Young children can't distinguish program content from commercials, especially when their favorite TV character is promoting a product.
- Shows like *Dora the Explorer* and *Diego* teach children both English and Spanish.
- Studies show that children who watch too much television are more likely to be overweight.
- Children tend to think that problems can be resolved in a half hour like they often are on television.
- Scientists from the University of Siena in Italy found that children experience a soothing effect by watching cartoons.

Writing

The principal of an elementary school asked you to write a short article that expresses your opinion about children and TV for the school newsletter. What is your opinion? Use your opinion as the topic sentence. Use your outline to help you write the paragraph.

_____

_____

_____

_____

_____

_____

_____

_____

_____

_____

_____

_____

Revising

A. Read your article and look for ways to improve it. Use the Revising Checklist on page 66 to help you.

B. Check for errors in grammar, spelling, and punctuation. Copy your revised paragraph on a separate piece of paper.

GRAMMAR GUIDE: RUN-ON SENTENCES

You have learned how to correct sentence fragments. Now you will learn how to correct another common problem, run-on sentences. A run-on sentence occurs when you write two complete sentences as one sentence.

**Example:** Sue loves to cook she is always in the kitchen.

There are several ways to correct run-on sentences. Study two common ways in the chart.

SOLUTION	EXAMPLE
Divide the run-on into two separate sentences. Use a period after each sentence.	Run-on sentence: Pat loves to swim he is often in the pool. Correct sentence: Pat loves to swim. He is often in the pool.
Use a coordinating conjunction (and, but, so) to make a compound sentence. Use a comma before the conjunction.	Run-on sentence: The movie was boring we watched it anyway. Correct sentence: The movie was boring, but we watched it anyway.

Correcting Run-on Sentences

Write *C* in front of each complete sentence. Write *R* in front of each run-on sentence. Then correct the run-on sentences.

__R__   1. I like my teacher she is very helpful.

I like my teacher. She is very helpful.

_____   2. This book is very confusing I can't understand it.

_____

_____   3. It was too hot to play tennis we decided to postpone the game.

_____

_____   4. Steve makes a lot of money, but he works too hard.

_____

_____   5. I enjoy going to restaurants, my husband prefers to eat at home.

_____

_____   6. Some people go to college full-time others go part-time.

_____

WRITING OPINION PARAGRAPHS

Writing Exercise 1

Prewriting

A. **Discuss the following topics in small groups. Talk about the pros and cons of each situation. Fill in the chart with your group's ideas. Then write a sentence that expresses your own personal opinion on each topic.**

1. mothers with small children working outside the house

PROS	CONS

Opinion statement: *In my opinion,* _____

_____

2. using nuclear power to solve the energy crisis

PROS	CONS

Opinion statement: _____

_____

3. using animals in laboratory experiments

PROS	CONS

Opinion statement: _____

_____

4. using the death penalty as a form of criminal punishment

PROS	CONS

Opinion statement: _____

_____

5. using cell phones while driving

PROS	CONS

Opinion statement: _____

_____

6. meeting people through online dating sites

PROS	CONS

Opinion statement: _____

_____

B. **Choose an opinion statement from Exercise A on page 133 to write about. Look at the ideas your group generated and add any other ideas that you think are important. Cross out ideas that you don't want to use.**

C. **Complete the outline. Choose three reasons for your main supporting points. Add details to strengthen each one. List your reasons in order of importance.**

Opinion Statement: _____

Reason 1: _____

Detail(s): _____

_____

Reason 2: _____

Detail(s): _____

_____

Reason 3: _____

Detail(s): _____

_____

Writing

Write the first draft of an opinion paragraph. Use your opinion statement as the topic sentence. Then use your reasons and details to support your opinion. Use some of the words from the box that signal order of importance that you learned in chapter 4. Remember, your purpose is to convince readers that your opinion is correct.

WORDS THAT SIGNAL ORDER OF IMPORTANCE		
first	also	one (way, reason, example)
first of all	in addition	another (way, reason, example)
for one thing	second	the next (way, reason, example)
most importantly	finally	the most important (way, reason, example)

_____

_____

_____

_____

_____

_____

_____

_____

_____

_____

_____

_____

_____

_____

Revising

A. **Read your paragraph and look for ways to improve it. As you revise your paragraph, think about these questions.**

1. Does the topic sentence state your opinion?

2. Do you have three reasons to support your opinion?

3. Do you have some details to make your paragraph more complete?

4. Have you used signal words to introduce your reasons?

5. Are there any irrelevant sentences?

B. **Check for errors in grammar, spelling, and punctuation. Copy your revised paragraph on a separate piece of paper.**

Writing Exercise 2

Prewriting

A. **Read the letter to the editor a woman sent to her local newspaper. Then discuss the letter in small groups.**

Dear Editor:

Last month our nine-year-old daughter was hit by a car. The man driving the car was drunk at the time and didn't stop at a stop sign. Our little girl was in the hospital for three long weeks. My husband and I didn't know if she would be able to walk again. It was a terrible time for us. Although today she is alive and well, we are afraid something like that might happen again.

Recently we heard that the punishment for the driver was only a $500 fine. He didn't go to jail, and he didn't lose his license. Today he is free to drive and possibly commit the same crime again. Maybe next time he will kill somebody.

We feel the laws against drinking and driving should be very strict. Drunk drivers should pay for their crimes. We think their licenses should be taken away. We need stricter laws!

Kathleen Johnson
Philadelphia, PA

B. **Discuss these questions with the people in your group.**

1. Do you think driving under the influence of alcohol is a serious crime?

    _____

2. Which of the following do you think is a fair punishment for people convicted of driving under the influence of alcohol? Why?

    _____ lose their license

    _____ be sent to jail

    _____ lose their car

    _____ pay a fine of $500 or more

    _____ other: _____

3. What is the punishment in your country?

Writing

Write the first draft of an opinion paragraph about drinking alcohol and driving.

_____

_____

_____

_____

_____

_____

_____

_____

_____

_____

Revising

A. **Revise your paragraph. Make sure all of your sentences support your opinion.**

B. **Copy your paragraph on a separate sheet of paper. Add this fact in the best place.**

The National Highway Traffic Safety Administration (NHTSA) estimates that 17,602 people were killed in alcohol-related traffic crashes in 2006, accounting for 41 percent of the total traffic fatalities for the year.

C. **Check for errors in grammar, spelling, and punctuation.**

Writing Exercise 3

Prewriting

Read the news article and study the police report. In small groups, discuss the situation and the three suspects. Together, decide who you think committed the crime.

Computer Crime Hits Local Bank

NATIONAL CITY BANK is the largest bank in the city. Its assets are in the billions of dollars. In 1980 the bank computerized its operations. The system had been trouble-free up until last Tuesday. On Wednesday, accountants discovered that a total of $800,000 was missing from several different accounts. It is not yet known where the funds were transferred. Police investigation has led to three possible suspects. These three people had access to the computer system that transferred the funds out of the bank.

POLICE REPORT

POSSIBLE SUSPECTS

(a) **Norman Glass**—computer operator
   - has worked at bank for 6 months
   - earns low salary
   - has wife and four children
   - lives in large house and drives expensive new car
   - before working at bank he served five years in army
     (won a Medal of Honor)

(b) **Richard Allen**—vice president of bank
   - has worked at bank 35 years
   - has a good history with bank
   - recently lost a lot of money in stock market
   - takes expensive vacations
   - earns very high salary

(c) **Jim Tomlin**— branch manager
   - has worked for bank 2 years
   - is active in church and community
   - graduated top of his class at Harvard
   - supports sick mother who lives in an expensive nursing home
   - has a gambling problem

Writing

Write a paragraph stating your opinion about who committed the crime. Be sure to give specific reasons to support your opinion.

_____

_____

_____

_____

_____

_____

_____

_____

Revising

A. Read your paragraph and look for ways to improve it. Use the Revising Checklist on page 66 to help you.

B. Check for errors in grammar, spelling, and punctuation. Copy your revised paragraph on a separate piece of paper.

Writing Exercise 4

Pretend you are the advice consultant for a newspaper. Write a response to the following letters. Then share your responses with your classmates.

1. Dear Adviser:

   My mother-in-law drives me crazy. She finds fault with everything I do. She doesn't think I take good care of my family. She criticizes my cooking and my housekeeping, as well as the way I am bringing up the children. My husband says I should just ignore her, but that is difficult because she lives across the street. What do you think I should do?

   Mrs. S.L.

Dear Mrs. S.L.:

_____

_____

_____

_____

_____

_____

   The Adviser

2. Dear Adviser:

   My roommate (and also my best friend) and I are having a problem. We have been sharing an apartment for three years and get along perfectly, except for one thing. She smokes cigarettes and I can't stand the smell. When I complained, she agreed to smoke only in her room with the window open. Unfortunately, I can still smell the smoke. I don't want to have to find another roommate, and I don't want to hurt her feelings. Do you have any suggestions?

   Confused

Dear Confused:

_____

_____

_____

_____

_____

   The Adviser

YOU BE THE EDITOR

Read the paragraph. It contains nine mistakes. Correct the mistakes. Copy the corrected paragraph on a separate piece of paper.

In my opinion, Suleiman was one of the greatest leaders of all time. He accomplished more than any others ruler of the Ottoman Empire. During his reign at 1520 to 1566, Suleiman expanding the size of the Ottoman Empire to include parts of Asia, europe, and Africa. While Suleimans military victorys made him a well-respected world leader, he did many another important things for the empire as well. For example, Suleiman introduced a new system of laws. He also promoted educate, architecture, and the arts. Therefore, I belief he deserves the name "Suleiman the Magnificent."

ON YOUR OWN

Write a paragraph giving your opinion on one of the following topics.
- marrying someone of a different religion
- following a vegetarian diet
- businesses caring only about making a profit
- enjoying your money when you earn it rather than saving it for the future
- good healthcare is a right, not a privilege
- meeting people online

COMPARING AND CONTRASTING

Very often in your writing you will need to explain how things are similar or different. When you *compare* two things, you explain how they are similar. When you *contrast* two things, you explain how they are different.

COMPARING

Read the paragraph and answer the questions.

Ann and Beth are identical twins, so it's easy to understand the embarrassing mistake I made yesterday. I was planning to ask Ann for a date, but it turned out I asked Beth. The two sisters look exactly alike. Ann is tall and thin with short, curly brown hair. Likewise, Beth is a tall, thin girl with short curly hair. They also have the same unusual blue-green eye color. In addition, Ann wears gold-rimmed glasses and so does Beth. Finally, both Ann and Beth have freckles. I wouldn't be surprised if they even have the exact same number of freckles. Now I have to explain my mistake to both of them.

1. What is the topic sentence?

    _____

2. What similarities about Ann and Beth does the author write about?

    _____   _____

    _____   _____

    _____   _____

SIGNAL WORDS OF COMPARISON

English has many words and sentence patterns to show comparisons.

A. Study the chart.

SIGNAL WORDS OF COMPARISON	EXAMPLES
*similarly	Tokyo has an efficient subway system. **Similarly**, London has an efficient subway system.
*likewise	Tokyo has an efficient subway system. **Likewise**, London has an efficient subway system.
both … and	**Both** London **and** Tokyo have efficient subway systems.
as + *adjective* + as as + *adverb* + as	Tokyo's subway system is **as** efficient **as** London's. Tokyo's subway system runs **as** efficiently **as** London's.
like	The weather in Philadelphia is **like** the weather in Istanbul.
the same + *noun* + as	My car is **the same** color **as** yours.
alike	Squash and racquetball are **alike** in several ways.
similar to	The population of Vienna is **similar to** the population of Frankfurt.

Similarly and *likewise* are used at the beginning of a sentence to signal to the reader that an idea expressed in that sentence is similar to an idea expressed in the previous sentence. Remember to use a comma after *similarly* or *likewise*.

B. Write sentences of comparison based on each pair of sentences. Use *similarly* or *likewise* in one sentence. Use a variety of other expressions for the other two sentences.

1. Soccer teams have eleven players. American football teams have eleven players.

    a. _Soccer teams have eleven players. Likewise, American football teams_
        have eleven players.
        Both soccer and American football teams have eleven players.

    b. _Soccer and American football teams have the same number of players._

2. Bats hibernate in winter. Bears hibernate in winter.

    a. _____

        _____

    b. _____

3. Learning to write well takes a lot of practice. Learning to drive a car takes a lot of practice.

   a. _____

   _____

   _____

   b. _____

4. Sunlight is a source of renewable energy. Wind is a source of renewable energy.

   a. _____

   _____

   b. _____

5. The weather in Moscow is cold. The weather in Anchorage is cold.

   a. _____

   _____

   b. _____

C. **Practice writing sentences using signal words for comparison.**

1. Danny weighs 185 pounds. Arthur weighs 185 pounds.

   (noun: *weight*) _Danny is the same weight as Arthur._

   (adjective: *heavy*) _Danny is as heavy as Arthur._

2. Mary is five feet tall. John is five feet tall.

   (noun: *height*) _____

   (adjective: *tall*) _____

3. This car costs $18,500. That car costs $18,500.

   (noun: *price*) _____

   (adjective: *expensive*) _____

4. My house has twelve rooms. Your house has twelve rooms.

    (noun: *size*) _____

    (adjective: *big*) _____

5. Jackson was born in 1982. Paul was born in 1982.

    (noun: *age*) _____

    (adjective: *old*) _____

6. This short story is seventy pages long. That story is seventy pages long.

    (noun: *length*) _____

    (adjective: *long*) _____

GRAMMAR GUIDE: SENTENCE PATTERNS OF COMPARISON

A. Now study these sentence patterns of comparison using *and* with *so, too, either,* and *neither*.

EXPLANATION	EXAMPLES
We use *so* or *too* with two affirmative sentences that express similar ideas. Use a comma before *and*.	Sentences with the verb be: Cathy is a medical student **and** Ashley **is too**. *Cathy is a medical student, **and so is** Ashley. Sentences with other verbs: Japan exports cars, **and** Germany **does too**. *Japan exports cars, **and so does** Germany.
We use *neither* or *not either* with negative sentences that express similar ideas.	Sentences with be: The blue dress isn't expensive, **and** the green dress **isn't either**. *The blue dress isn't expensive, **and neither is** the green dress. Sentences with other verbs: Owls don't sleep at night, **and** mice **don't either**. *Owls don't sleep at night, **and neither do** mice.

* Notice the word order in sentences with *so* and *neither*. The subject comes after the verb.

B. **Practice using these structures. Follow the example.**

1. Judy runs four miles a day. Her roommate runs four miles a day.

   a. _Judy runs four miles a day, and her roommate does, too._

   b. _Judy runs four miles a day, and so does her roommate._

2. Mark plays the piano. Dave plays the piano.

   a. _____

   b. _____

3. The bank opens at 9 A.M. The grocery store opens at 9 A.M.

   a. _____

   b. _____

4. Jamaica is sunny and beautiful. Hawaii is sunny and beautiful.

   a. _____

   b. _____

5. Peter doesn't smoke. Alex doesn't smoke.

   a. _____

   b. _____

6. Skiing is an exciting sport. Surfing is an exciting sport.

   a. _____

   b. _____

7. The Browns don't have a car. The Johnsons don't have a car.

   a. _____

   b. _____

8. Philadelphia is an old city. Boston is an old city.

   a. _____

   b. _____

9. Suzanne lives in a small apartment. Dave lives in a small apartment.

   a. _____

   b. _____

10. Charlie isn't friendly. Liz isn't friendly.

a. _____

b. _____

11. Children need love. Adults need love.

a. _____

b. _____

12. Maria doesn't have a driver's license. Orhan doesn't have a driver's license.

a. _____

b. _____

Writing Topic Sentences for Comparison Paragraphs

When you write the topic sentence for a comparison paragraph, you must state the two things that you are comparing. Look at the following topic sentences.

- Time Out and The Blue Gills are very similar bands.
- My two favorite bands, Time Out and The Blue Gills, have several things in common.
- The rock bands Time Out and The Blue Gills are alike in many ways.
- Time Out and The Blue Gills share many similarities.
- Time Out is similar to The Blue Gills in several ways.

Write a topic sentence for each of the following paragraphs.

1. _____ First of all, both cities are hot and humid most of the year. The typical daytime temperature in both places is about 92 degrees Fahrenheit (33 degrees Celsius) with humidity of 99 percent. It also rains a lot during the summer in Hill View. Likewise, it rains almost every day in Valley Ridge in the summer. Finally, the evenings and nights are warm in both places.

2. _____ The main similarity is that both dogs are very friendly. Spot loves people, and so does Freckles. In addition, both of my dogs are smart and can do lots of tricks. For example, both can roll over on command. Another similarity is that both dogs are picky eaters. They only like the most expensive dog food.

3. _____ First of all, they have many of the same sections. For example, The Reporter and The Monitor both have sections on politics, finance, science, and culture. In addition, both of these popular magazines cost $7.99, and both are read by millions of people around the world. They also have the same cover story almost every week, and they usually review the same books and movies in their culture sections. Another similarity between the two magazines is their point of view. The Reporter is very conservative, and so is The Monitor. Finally, both magazines are available online.

Writing Exercise 1

Prewriting

Write four sentences comparing Stephanie Brooks and Ann Friedman. Base your comparisons on the information provided on their driver's licenses.

1. _____

2. _____

3. _____

4. _____

Writing

Use your sentences to write the first draft of a paragraph comparing Stephanie and Ann. Remember to begin with a topic sentence and use some transitions that show comparison.

_____

_____

_____

_____

_____

_____

_____

Revising

A. Read your paragraph and look for ways to improve it. Use the Revising Checklist on page 66 to help you.

B. Check for errors in grammar, spelling, and punctuation. Copy your revised paragraph on a separate piece of paper.

Writing Exercise 2

Prewriting

Study the following ads. Write four sentences of comparison based on your observations and the information provided.

1. _____

2. _____

3. _____

4. _____

Writing

Use your sentences to write the first draft of a paragraph comparing the two sweatshirts.

_____

_____

_____

_____

_____

_____

_____

Revising

A. Read your paragraph and look for ways to improve it. Use the Revising Checklist on page 66 to help you.

B. Check for errors in grammar, spelling, and punctuation. Copy your revised paragraph on a separate piece of paper.

Writing Exercise 3

Prewriting

A. **Study this biographical information about two important Americans, John Adams and Thomas Jefferson.**

John Adams

Born: October 19, 1735
Died: July 4, 1826
- important person in the American Revolution
- delegate to the Continental Congress
- signer of Declaration of Independence
- studied and practiced law
- second U.S. president
- father of the sixth U.S. president—John Quincy Adams

Thomas Jefferson

Born: April 13, 1743
Died: July 4, 1826
- played important role in American Revolution
- delegate to the Continental Congress
- author and signer of Declaration of Independence
- third president of United States
- foreign minister to France
- founded University of Virginia
- studied and practiced law
- philosopher, architect, inventor

B. **Make a list of the similarities between the two men.**

_____   _____

_____   _____

_____   _____

C. **Write a topic sentence for your paragraph.**

_____

Writing

Write the first draft of a paragraph comparing Adams and Jefferson. Use your list of similarities as a guide.

_____

_____

_____

_____

_____

_____

_____

_____

_____

_____

_____

Revising

A. Read your paragraph and look for ways to improve it. Use the Revising Checklist on page 66 to help you.

B. Check for errors in grammar, spelling, and punctuation. Copy your revised paragraph on a separate piece of paper.

Writing Exercise 4

Prewriting

A. Choose one of the following topics to compare. Brainstorm a list of similarities between the two things you are comparing.

- two movies you have seen
- two professional athletes you admire
- two restaurants you have been to
- two teachers you have had
- two sports you enjoy
- two people you know

_____   _____

_____   _____

_____   _____

B. Write a topic sentence for your paragraph. Be sure to identify the two things you are comparing.

_____

_____

Writing

Write the first draft of a paragraph of comparison. Use your list of similarities as a guide. Use *similarly* or *likewise* in at least one sentence.

_____

_____

_____

_____

_____

_____

_____

_____

_____

Revising

A. **Look for ways to improve your paragraph. Think about these questions.**

1. Are there any other similarities you should include?
2. Can you add a concluding sentence?
3. Did you use enough signal words?
4. Did you use *similarly* and *likewise* correctly?

B. **Check for errors in grammar, spelling, and punctuation. Copy your revised paragraph on a separate piece of paper.**

CONTRASTING

When you describe the differences between two people, places, or things, you are contrasting them.

A. **Read the paragraph.**

> When Michael was in Sedona last week, he ate at two very different restaurants. He had lunch at Cantina Italiana and dinner at the Cityside Café. First of all, the food at Cantina was delicious, but the food at Cityside was terrible. The atmosphere at Cantina Italiana was much better than the one at Cityside. Cantina was clean and quiet. However, the Cityside Café was dirty and noisy. In addition, while the server at the Cantina Italiana was attentive and polite, the server at Cityside was rude. Finally, although the meal at Cantina was more expensive than the meal at Cityside, it was worth the price. Michael will always remember his delicious lunch at Cantina Italiana, but he can't wait to forget his terrible dinner at Cityside Café.

B. **Make a list of the differences between the two restaurants.**

_____	_____
_____	_____
_____	_____

SIGNAL WORDS OF CONTRAST

English uses special sentence patterns and signal words to show contrast.

SIGNAL WORDS OF CONTRAST	EXAMPLES
However, *in contrast*, and *on the other hand* are used at the beginning of a sentence to signal to the reader that an idea expressed in that sentence is being contrasted with an idea in the previous sentence. Use a comma after these words and phrases.	In South Africa, red is the color of mourning. **However**, in China, red is the color of good luck. In South Africa, red is the color of mourning. **On the other hand**, in China, red is the color of good luck. In South Africa, red is the color of mourning. **In contrast**, in China, red is the color of good luck.
While, *whereas*, and *but* are used to show contrast between two clauses in one sentence. *While* and *whereas* can be used at the beginning or in the middle of a sentence. *But* is used in the middle of a sentence. Use a comma to separate the clauses.	Dr. Meng specializes in surgery, **while** Dr. Becker specializes in internal medicine. **While** Dr. Becker specializes in internal medicine, Dr. Meng specializes in surgery. Dr. Meng specializes in surgery, **whereas** Dr. Becker specializes in internal medicine. **Whereas** Dr. Becker specializes in internal medicine, Dr. Meng specializes in surgery. Dr. Becker specializes in internal medicine, **but** Dr. Meng specializes in surgery.
Different from and *unlike* are used to show contrast between two nouns. *Different from* is used in the middle of a sentence. *Unlike* often is used at the beginning of a sentence.	My mother's personality is **different from** my father's personality. **Unlike** my mother, my father is quiet.

A. Use a variety of sentence patterns and signal words to connect the following sentences.

1. I am usually punctual. My brother is often late.

    a. _____

    b. _____

    c. _____

2. In Egypt and Burma, yellow signifies mourning. White means mourning in China and Japan.

    a. _____

    b. _____

    c. _____

3. In the United States, people drive on the right side of the road. In Turkey, people drive on the left side of the road.

    a. _____

    b. _____

    c. _____

4. Some mushrooms are edible and safe to eat. Other mushrooms are poisonous and should be avoided.

    a. _____

    b. _____

    c. _____

B. Add signal words that show contrast in the following paragraphs.

1.   Sunny English Institute (SEI) in Miami, Florida, is _____ Rocky Mountain English Program (RMEP) in Denver, Colorado, in several ways. First of all, the tuition at SEI is very expensive. _____, the tuition at RMEP is more reasonable. Secondly, _____ RMEP is a small school, SEI is a very big school. The program at SEI is two months. _____, the program at RMEP is only five weeks. Finally, SEI includes a TOEFL preparation class, _____ RMEP does not.

2. There are several spelling differences between British English and American English. For example, _____ certain nouns end in *-our* in British English, such as *colour, honour, humour,* and *labour,* these words end in *-or* in American English: *color, honor, humor,* and *labor.* Also, some verbs end in *-ise* in British English, such as *specialise, recognise,* and *patronise.* _____, they end in *-ize* in American English: *specialize, recognize,* and *patronize.*

3. My friend Lily has a very specific diet. She is a vegan, which is not the same thing as being a vegetarian. Vegans are much stricter than vegetarians. Naturally, vegans do not eat meat, fish, or poultry. _____ unlike vegetarians, who eat animal byproducts such as eggs, milk, and butter, vegans do not eat dairy foods or any animal byproducts at all. In fact, some vegans will not even eat honey because it comes from bees, _____ vegetarians who are not vegan usually will. Vegans avoid using products that have been tested on animals. Most vegans, like my friend Lily, love animals and feel that being a vegan is one way to help protect animals.

G. Work in groups of four. Complete the chart with information about yourself and the people in your group. Then write sentences that compare or contrast the people in your group.

NAMES	What is your favorite color?	What is your favorite food?	What is your favorite kind of music?	What sports do you like?
Your name:				

1. _____
2. _____
3. _____
4. _____
5. _____
6. _____

GRAMMAR GUIDE: COMPARATIVE ADJECTIVES

Adjectives that are used to show the difference between two things are called comparative adjectives. Comparative adjectives are often followed by *than*.

A.   To write sentences with comparative adjectives, follow these rules.

RULES	EXAMPLES	SENTENCES
Add *-er* to adjectives that have one syllable. (Note: double the final consonant if it is preceded by a vowel.)	light ⟶ light**er** big ⟶ big**ger**	A feather is **lighter than** a rock. Abu Dhabi is **bigger than** Ajman.
Add *-ier* to adjectives that have two syllables and end in *y*.	funny ⟶ funn**ier**	My joke was **funnier than** your joke.
Use *more* in front of adjectives that have two or more syllables	interesting ⟶ **more** interesting	I think biology is **more interesting than** physics.

Notice these common exceptions:

- good ⟶ better
- well ⟶ better
- bad ⟶ worse
- far ⟶ farther, further

B.   Read the paragraph and underline the comparative adjectives.

Sue and Linda are sisters, but they are different in many ways. For one thing, their physical appearances are very different. Sue is taller and thinner than Linda. Linda has darker eyes and longer hair than Sue. Their personalities are also different. Sue is more serious and more ambitious than Linda. She is a better student because she studies harder than her sister. On the other hand, Linda is more creative and more social than Sue.

C.   Practice using comparative adjectives. Follow the example.

1.   Gary weighs 178 pounds. Gerald weighs 165 pounds. (heavy)

   Gary is heavier than Gerald.

2.   The Nile is 4,145 miles long. The Amazon is 3,915 miles long. (long)

   _____

3.   The Pacific Ocean is 36,198 feet deep. The Atlantic Ocean is 28,374 feet deep. (deep)

   _____

4.   The third chapter is very difficult. The fourth chapter isn't as difficult. (difficult)

   _____

5. The black dress is $75. The purple dress is $120. (expensive)

_____

6. Mount Everest is 29,025 feet high. Mount Fuji is 12,389 feet high. (high)

_____

Writing Topic Sentences for Contrast Paragraphs

When you write the topic sentence for a contrast paragraph, you must state the two things that you are contrasting.

A. **Look at the following list of sample topic sentences.**
- *The Reporter* and *Style* are different types of weekly magazines.
- *The Reporter* and *Style* are different in many ways.
- *The Reporter* and *Style* have many differences.
- *The Reporter* and *Style* differ in several ways.

B. **Write a topic sentence for each of the following paragraphs.**

1. _____ First of all, the temperature in Westland is usually hotter than it is in Eastfalls. In Westland it is often in the nineties, but in Eastfalls, the temperature rarely goes above 80. Secondly, the humidity is much higher in Westland than it is in Eastfalls. This makes it much more uncomfortable to be outdoors in Westland. Finally, it rains a lot in Westland; however, it is usually dry in Eastfalls. Overall, the weather in Eastfalls is more pleasant.

2. _____ For one thing, they are different in appearance. Fluffy is a small, curly-haired dog, but Shane is big and shaggy. Another difference is seen in their personalities. Fluffy is very friendly and loves people. On the other hand, Shane is shy and afraid of people. Finally, my two dogs differ in their intelligence. Unlike Shane, Fluffy is smart and can do lots of tricks.

3. _____ First of all, *The Reporter* comes out once a week, but *Style* only comes out once a month. Secondly, the two magazines have different sections. *The Reporter* has sections on politics, finance, science, and culture. On the other hand, *Style* has sections on fashion, home decorating, cooking, and gardening. In addition, *The Reporter* is less expensive. It costs $6 per issue, but *Style* costs $8 per issue. Finally, *The Reporter* is available in print and online; however, *Style* is only in available in print.

PARAGRAPH POINTER: Compare/Contrast

When you choose two things to compare or contrast, make sure the two things belong to the same general category. For example, you could compare/contrast two friends, two songs, two types of computers. But you should not compare/contrast cars and computers. You could, however, compare and contrast cars and motorcycles.

WRITING PARAGRAPHS OF CONTRAST

Writing Exercise 1

Prewriting

A. You and your friend are looking for an apartment to share near campus. You saw these two descriptions of apartments on the Internet. Read the descriptions.

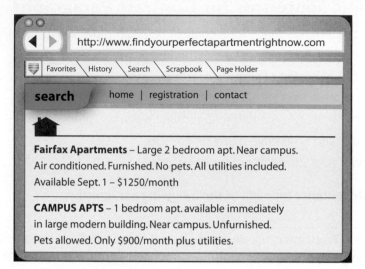

Fairfax Apartments – Large 2 bedroom apt. Near campus. Air conditioned. Furnished. No pets. All utilities included. Available Sept. 1 – $1250/month

CAMPUS APTS – 1 bedroom apt. available immediately in large modern building. Near campus. Unfurnished. Pets allowed. Only $900/month plus utilities.

B. Write four sentences contrasting the two apartments.

1. _____

2. _____

3. _____

4. _____

Writing

Which apartment would you choose? Write the first draft of a paragraph explaining your decision and the differences between the two apartments.

_____

_____

_____

_____

_____

_____

Revising

A. Read your paragraph and look for ways to improve it. Use the Revising Checklist on page 66 to help you.

B. Check for errors in grammar, spelling, and punctuation. Copy your revised paragraph on a separate piece of paper.

Writing Exercise 2

Prewriting

A. **You and a friend are planning a trip to Hawaii. You found these advertisements in the newspaper. Read the advertisements.**

PLAN A

Hawaiian **FLING**

Price : **$1,799**

Length : 8 days, 7 nights

Includes:
Airfare from Los Angeles to Honolulu
Welcome party
Visit two islands: Waikiki and Oahu
Breakfast and dinner
Three-star hotel accommodations
Transportation to and from airport

PLAN B

Dream Vacation in
HAWAII

Price: **$2599**

Length: 10 days, 9 nights

Includes:
• Airfare from Los Angeles to Honolulu
• Welcome party
• Visit three islands: Waikiki, Oahu, Maui
• Breakfast, lunch, and dinner
• Deluxe 5-star hotel accommodations
• Guided tours around each island
• Transportation to and from airport

B. **Make a list of differences between the two trips.**

_____   _____

_____   _____

_____   _____

_____   _____

Writing

Write a one-paragraph e-mail message to your friend contrasting the two plans and suggesting the one you think would be better for you.

Send	Reply	Forward	Move	Print	Delete	▲ ▼

Subject: Hawaii trip

From:

To: mypal@anyschool.edu

Revising

A. Read your e-mail and look for ways to improve it. Use the Revising Checklist on page 66 to help you.

B. Check for errors in grammar, spelling, and punctuation. Copy your revised e-mail on a separate piece of paper.

Writing Exercise 3

Prewriting

A. You are hiring a new English instructor for your school. You received the following two résumés from people applying for the job. Study the résumés.

Lynn Whitnall
Plaza de la Paz, No.2
CP 36000 Guanajuato
Gto, Mexico
+52 (473) 732-02-13
l.whitnall@email.com

POSITION DESIRED:
English instructor

EDUCATION
1995 BA Spanish, New York University

EMPLOYMENT
2000–present, Spanish teacher, International
                          High School

1997–2000   English Instructor, Tokyo Girls
                          High School

1995–1997   Peace Corps volunteer in
                          Colombia

OTHER
Fluent in Spanish, French, Japanese

AWARDS
Excellence in Teaching Award, 2004

Debra Fines
42 St. James Place
Philadelphia, PA 19106
(215) 555-9008
debraf@bestmail.net

Position Desired:
English Instructor

Education:
1993–97   BA English, McGill University
1998   MA English, University of Toronto
2000   PhD Linguistics, University of Pennsylvania

Employment Experience
2005–present   Consultant and Author
2000–2005   Instructor, Intensive English Program,
                              University of Vermont
1999–2000   Teaching Assistant, Linguistics Department,
                              University of Pennsylvania
1998–1999   Swimming Teacher
1993–1998   Server, *Chez Robert*

Publication:
English Verb Tenses, Shortman Publishing Company, 2006

Personal:
Fluent in French; competitive swimmer

B. Write four sentences of contrast based on the information in the résumés.

1. _Debra has more education than Lynn._

2. _____

3. _____

4. _____

Writing

Who would you hire for the job? Write a paragraph supporting your decision.

_____

_____

_____

_____

_____

_____

Revising

A. Read your paragraph and look for ways to improve it. Use the Revising Checklist on page 66 to help you.

B. Check for errors in grammar, spelling, and punctuation. Copy your revised paragraph on a separate piece of paper.

Writing Exercise 4

Prewriting

A. Talk to a classmate from another country. Discuss the differences between your two cultures. If everyone in the class is from the same country, discuss the differences between your family and your partner's family. Discuss these topics.

- eating habits
- climate
- social customs
- family life
- education
- political system

B. Choose one of the topics to write about. Make a list of the differences.

_____   _____

_____   _____

_____   _____

C. Write a topic sentence. Include the topic (education, family life, etc.) you are contrasting and the names of the two countries.

Example: There are several differences in social customs between Peru and Taiwan.

_____

Writing

Write the first draft of a paragraph of contrast. Use your list as a guide. Start with the biggest differences.

_____

_____

_____

_____

_____

_____

_____

_____

Revising

A. Exchange paragraphs with a partner. Ask your partner for suggestions to improve your paragraph and give suggestions to improve your partner's paragraph. You can also use the Revising Checklist on page 66 to help you.

B. Check for errors in grammar, spelling, and punctuation. Copy your revised paragraph on a separate piece of paper.

YOU BE THE EDITOR

The e-mail message has nine mistakes. Correct the mistakes. Copy the corrected message on a separate piece of paper.

| Send | Reply | Forward | Move | Print | Delete | ▲ | ▼ |

Subject: Madrid and Barcelona

From:

To: myfriend@institute.edu

Hi,

This is just a short message to let you know that we are back from my trip to Spain. was a great vacation. Here is a picture of us outside our hotel. We went to madrid and Barcelona. Both is great cities, and I was surprise at the differences between them. First of all, the cultures are different and the people speak differents dialects. Madrid is also more bigger and busiest than Barcelona. Madrid is more crowded to Barcelona. Luckily, the weather was sunny, warm, and beautiful in Barcelona, but it rained the whole time we were in Madrid!

Now that I am back, let's set a date for the next committee meeting.

Jane

A. **Choose one of the following topics to write about. You may write about either the similarities or the differences.**

- two cities you have visited
- two vacations you have taken
- two jobs you have had
- two athletic teams you like
- two types of music
- an online course and a traditional course

B. **Write a paragraph comparing Benjamin Franklin and Thomas Jefferson. Use the information that follows as well as the information on page 150.**

Benjamin Franklin 1706–1790

- founded University of Pennsylvania
- helped write Declaration of Independence
- important person in American Revolution
- well-known philosopher and thinker
- ambassador to France

ANALYZING CAUSES AND EFFECTS

Most situations, events, and actions have causes and effects. For example, when you explain *why* something happened, or *why* you made a certain decision, you are describing the causes or reasons. On the other hand, when you explain the results of something that happened, or the results of a decision you made, you are describing the effects. In this chapter, you will learn how to write about the causes and effects of a situation.

Read the paragraph. Circle the topic sentence. Underline the three main reasons the student gives for taking a year off from college.

I've decided to take a year off from college for several reasons. First of all, I need to work for a while because the tuition has gone up. Paying the tuition and living in the dorm is very expensive. I know I can save money by living at home and working. In addition, I need time away from school to think about my major. Since I'm not really sure what career path I want to pursue, I don't want to waste time and money taking the wrong courses. Most importantly, I just need a break from the stress of school. I was feeling a lot of pressure to get high grades and excel at everything at school. I was also getting headaches and stomachaches due to all the stress. I haven't made my decision lightly, but I hope it is the right one.

UNDERSTANDING CAUSES AND EFFECTS

Look at the sets of pictures. The first picture in each set shows a cause. The second picture shows an effect. Write a sentence that describes each picture.

1. Cause: _The man found $100._ Effect: _He is happy._

2. Cause: _____ Effect: _____

_____ _____

3. Cause: _____ Effect: _____

_____ _____

4. Cause: _____   Effect: _____

    _____   _____

SIGNAL WORDS OF CAUSE

English uses special sentence patterns and signal words to express causes.

Study the chart.

SIGNAL WORDS THAT INTRODUCE CAUSES	EXAMPLES
Because and ***since*** introduce a clause that states a reason or cause of something. The cause clause can come at the beginning of a sentence or at the end of a sentence. Use a comma if the clause that begins with ***because*** or ***since*** comes at the beginning of a sentence.	I took my umbrella **because** it was raining. **Because** it was raining, I took my umbrella. I took my umbrella **since** it was raining. **Since** it was raining, I took my umbrella.
Due to and ***because of*** introduce a noun phrase that states a cause. The cause phrase can come in the middle of the sentence or at the beginning of a sentence. Use a comma if the phrase that begins with ***because of*** or ***due to*** comes at the beginning of a sentence.	I took my umbrella **due to** the rain. **Due to** the rain, I took my umbrella. I took my umbrella **because of** the rain. **Because of** the rain, I took my umbrella.

WRITING SENTENCES OF CAUSE

A. **Write a sentence of cause for each of the sets of pictures on pages 166–167. Use *because* or *since*.**

1. _The boy is happy because he found $100._

2. _____

3. _____

4. _____

B. **Complete the sentences.**

1. I am learning English because _____

   _____

2. Due to the drought, _____

   _____

3. _____

   _____ because of the

   crisis in the economy.

4. Since my job is very stressful, _____

   _____

5. Gabe raised his hand because _____

   _____

6. Since I can't read Japanese fluently, _____

   _____

7. _____

   _____ due to the high

   rate of unemployment.

C. **Work with a partner. The questions in column A are all jokes. Match the questions with the answers in column B. Then write a sentence for each one using** *because* **or** *since.*

A	B
____ 1. Why did the man cross the street?	a. Its head is so far from its body.
____ 2. Why did the man throw the clock out the window?	b. They live in schools.
____ 3. Why does the giraffe have such a long neck?	c. He wanted to see time fly.
____ 4. Why did the man tiptoe past the medicine cabinet?	d. He wanted to get to the other side.
____ 5. Why are fish smarter than insects?	e. He didn't want to wake up the sleeping pills.
____ 6. Why is a library the tallest building?	f. It has the largest number of stories.

1. _____

2. _____

3. _____

4. _____

5. _____

6. _____

WRITING TOPIC SENTENCES FOR PARAGRAPHS ABOUT CAUSES

When you write a paragraph about causes, your topic sentence should include the situation (decision, event, etc.) and the number of causes. You can use expressions such as *several reasons, three main causes, two major reasons,* etc.

Here are some examples of topic sentences for paragraphs about causes.

- I decided to move to New York for several reasons.
- The economy is doing well for three main reasons.
- There are several causes of diabetes in adults.

Write topic sentences for the following paragraphs.

1. _____ Some people move because they want to find better jobs or to advance their careers. Others are attracted to new places because the weather is better. Still others want to move to a place with less crime. Finally, people often want to move to a place with a lower cost of living. For these reasons, every year millions of people pack up and move to new places.

2. _____ One reason so many American children are overweight is that they eat too much junk food that is high in calories, sugar, and fat. Another reason is that many children do not get enough exercise. Because they spend so much time sitting in front of the television set or playing computer games, they do not move around very much. Genetics is another reason that children become overweight. Children whose parents or brothers or sisters are overweight may be at an increased risk of becoming overweight themselves.

3. _____ First of all, our soccer team had a great coach. He inspired us to play our best and gave us a lot of helpful advice. Another reason we won the tournament was due to our loyal fans. They came to all of our games and cheered us on. Without their support we probably wouldn't have won. Most importantly, we owe our success to our team spirit. Because we worked and practiced hard as a team, we were able to achieve our goal and win the tournament.

4. _____ One reason is that the English spelling system is very irregular. Many words sound the same but are spelled differently. For example, *hear* and *here* sound the same but are spelled differently. In addition, many of the grammar rules are complicated. For every rule it seems that there are two exceptions. Finally, English is difficult to master because it has so many idioms. In fact, native speakers commonly use more than 8,000 idioms!

WRITING PARAGRAPHS ABOUT CAUSES

Writing Exercise 1

Prewriting

Over the past 150 years there has been a huge increase in population. Read the list of causes and discuss them in small groups.

- advances in medicine and health care
- better sanitation
- improved farming methods that produce more and better food
- fewer infant deaths and more people living longer

Writing

Use the list to write a paragraph about the causes of the population increase. Begin with a topic sentence and include signal words.

_____

_____

_____

_____

_____

_____

_____

_____

Revising

A. Read the paragraph you wrote. Look for ways to improve it. Use the Revising Checklist on page 66 to help you.

B. Check for errors in grammar, spelling, and punctuation. Rewrite your revised paragraph on a separate piece of paper.

Writing Exercise 2

Prewriting

A. **Think of an important decision you have made or choose one of the following:**
- getting married
- choosing your major
- accepting/quitting a job
- buying a house
- moving to another country
- having a baby

Decision: _____

B. **Why did you make your decision? Make a list of reasons that influenced your decision.**

_____   _____

_____   _____

C. **Write a topic sentence for your paragraph.**

_____

Writing

Write the first draft of your paragraph. Use your list of reasons as a guide.

_____

_____

_____

_____

_____

_____

_____

_____

_____

_____

Revising

A. **Exchange paragraphs with a classmate. Give each other suggestions for improving your paragraphs. You can use the Revising Checklist on page 66 to help you.**

B. **Use your partner's ideas to improve your paragraph. Also, consider these questions.**

1. Do all of your reasons relate to the decision stated in the topic sentence?

2. Are your reasons in a logical order? Did you include signal words?

C. Check for errors in grammar, spelling, and punctuation. Copy your revised paragraph on a separate piece of paper.

Writing Exercise 3

Prewriting

Situation: You are a business administration student. You have been asked to analyze the following case with a group of students.

A. **Read the case.**

CASE #6

On September 5, Michael Williams opened a small music store selling compact discs. The store is located next to the lobby on the ground floor of the Fairfax Apartment Building. The apartment building is on a small side street just outside of town. It is 3 miles away from a shopping center that has two large music stores.

Mr. Williams spent $15,000 buying CDs for his shop. Most of the CDs were hip-hop and rock. He sold each CD for $15. He hired two people to work as sales clerks and paid them $8.50 an hour. The shop was open Monday to Friday from 1 to 5 P.M. Mr. Williams would not accept checks or credit cards.

On December 19, Mr. Williams closed his shop. He put a sign on the door that said "Out of Business."

B. **Discuss this case in your group. Why do you think the business failed? Make a list of at least four causes. You will add more later.**

_____

_____

_____

_____

_____

_____

_____

_____

C. **Now study this graph and answer the questions.**

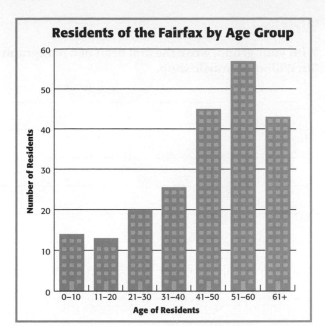

Residents of the Fairfax by Age Group

1. How would you describe the people who live in the Fairfax? What generalization can you make about the people?

_____

_____

_____

2. Can you use the information in this graph to think of another cause of the failure of this business? Add it to your list of causes on page 172.

D. **Now study the following table. Write three statements based on the table.**

NUMBER OF PEOPLE WHO WALK PAST THE STORE							
	MON	TUES	WED	THURS	FRI	SAT	SUN
8 A.M.–12 P.M.	30	35	28	29	31	32	20
12 P.M.–6 P.M.	10	12	16	15	20	70	65
6 P.M.–12 A.M.	40	47	53	42	60	65	40

1. _____

2. _____

3. _____

E. **Does the information in this table show another cause of the failure? What is it? Add it to your list of causes on page 172.**

F. **Look over your list of causes. Can you think of any others? Are there any you want to cross out?**

Writing

With your group, write the first draft of a paragraph explaining the failure of Mr. Williams's music shop.

_____

_____

_____

_____

_____

_____

_____

_____

_____

_____

_____

Revising

A. **Read your paragraph and look for ways to improve it. Use the Revising Checklist on page 66 to help you. Also, think about these questions.**

1. Do all of your causes help explain why Mr. Williams's compact disc shop failed?

2. Are your causes in a logical order?

3. Did you include signal words?

B. **Check for other errors. Copy your revised paragraph on a separate piece of paper.**

WRITING ABOUT EFFECTS

Read the paragraph. Underline the topic sentence and answer the questions that follow.

Taking a salsa dance class has had many positive effects on my life. One of the first things I noticed was the physical effect. As a result of taking this class, I am in much better shape. For example, my posture and coordination are better. Salsa dancing requires a lot of physical energy and burns a lot of calories, so I've lost several pounds. Another effect is that I have more self-confidence. Consequently, my social skills have improved and I've become more outgoing. Finally, I've met a lot of great people taking salsa classes. This leads to the biggest effect on my life. I'm engaged to marry a great guy that I met in the class!

1. What effects does the author give?

   _____

   _____

2. What was the biggest effect?

   _____

SIGNAL WORDS THAT INTRODUCE EFFECTS

English uses special sentence patterns and signal words to express effects.

SIGNAL WORDS THAT INTRODUCE EFFECTS	EXAMPLES
We use **therefore**, **thus**, **consequently**, and **as a result** to show a cause/effect relationship between two complete sentences. These words introduce the effect, which is always stated in the second sentence. Use a comma after these words.	Our company is expanding rapidly. **Therefore**, we hired more people. Our company is expanding rapidly. **Consequently**, we hired more people. Our company is expanding rapidly. **As a result**, we hired more people.
We also use **so** to show a cause/effect relationship. **So** combines two sentences into one. Use a comma before **so**.	Our company is expanding rapidly, **so** we hired more people.

Writing Sentences of Cause and Effect

A. **Write a sentence of cause and effect using *so* or *therefore* for each of the sets of pictures on pages 166–167.**

1. _The young man found $100. Therefore, he is happy._____

2. _____

3. _____

4. _____

B. **Match the causes and effects.**

Effects	Causes
__d__ 1. I'm going skiing today.	**a.** It was faster than the train.
_____ 2. We moved to the country.	**b.** He likes to get exercise in the morning.
_____ 3. We bought a new car.	**c.** The city was too crowded.
_____ 4. They took an airplane.	**d.** It snowed five inches last night.
_____ 5. She doesn't eat desserts.	**e.** It didn't rain enough this summer.
_____ 6. The flowers in our garden died.	**f.** The old one used too much gas.
_____ 7. We turned on the air conditioner.	**g.** She's on a diet.
_____ 8. He rides his bike to work.	**h.** It is very hot today.

C. **Now combine the causes and effects to make new sentences. Use *so, because,* or *therefore*.**

1.   It snowed five inches last night, so I'm going skiing today.

2.   _____

3.   _____

4.   _____

5.   _____

6.   _____

7.   _____

8.   _____

WRITING TOPIC SENTENCES FOR PARAGRAPHS ABOUT EFFECTS

The topic sentence for a paragraph about effects should state the situation, decision, and event and indicate that you will be discussing its effects. Here are some examples of topic sentences for paragraphs about effects.

- Computers have had several important effects on society.
- There are a number of consequences of global warming.
- The birth of my twins has had several effects on my life.
- The flood caused several problems in our town.

Write topic sentences for the following paragraphs.

1.   _____ For one
thing, there was so much snow that it was dangerous to drive. Most of the side streets were impassable, and several main roads had to be closed. Even the mail was delayed. Students had the day off because all the schools in the area were closed. Many stores and businesses were closed as well. Finally, the snowstorm cost the city a lot of money to remove the snow and plow the roads.

2. _____ First of
all, running on a regular basis benefits your body. For example, it can increase the efficiency of your heart and lungs. Running also helps the body develop greater physical endurance. It enables your body to become more mechanically efficient and can improve your physical coordination. Finally, running has psychological benefits. It can improve your mood and lower your stress level.

3. _____ Some studies
show that listening to music can increase a child's verbal and emotional intelligence. It can also improve concentration and stimulate creative thinking. Some scientists think music can even improve children's memory. Finally, music can relax children and make them feel more comfortable. Overall, it seems that music is beneficial to children's learning and sense of well-being.

IRRELEVANT SENTENCES

PARAGRAPH POINTER: Paragraph Unity

Remember that an important characteristic of a good paragraph is that it has unity. That means all the supporting sentences must relate to the main idea stated in the topic sentence. Any sentence that does not support the main idea is an *irrelevant sentence* and does not belong in the paragraph.

The following paragraphs each contain one sentence that is irrelevant. Cross out that sentence and explain to a partner why it does not belong.

1. There are several reasons why many American women are waiting until they are thirty years old or older to have their first baby. Some women have good jobs and want to continue their careers. Many American couples have two children. Other women don't want the responsibility of having children until they are older. Still others are waiting until they are financially secure before they start a family. Increased personal and professional opportunities for women often result in delaying motherhood.

2. Watching television can have several positive effects on students learning English. One effect is that students can improve their pronunciation by listening to the people talking on television. Many commercials are too long and interrupt interesting shows. In addition, students see how native speakers interact while they are talking. As a result, they can observe the gestures and natural body language that are part of communication. Most importantly, because the people on TV use so many idioms, students will hear them used in context. This will help students better understand the meanings of idioms.

3. The introduction of affordable automobiles had several effects on society. First of all, automobiles created a more mobile society. Cars made it possible for people to move out of the cities and into the suburbs. Automobiles also affected the growth of new businesses. Gas stations, auto repair shops, and roadside restaurants became necessary. Railroads had a great effect on society, too. In addition, new roads were built as a result of the increase in the number of cars. All of these changes meant that the automobile transformed the lifestyle of millions of people.

WRITING PARAGRAPHS ABOUT EFFECTS

Writing Exercise 1

Prewriting

A. **Think about this topic:** There are several effects of global warming.

B. **What effects can you and your classmates think of? Brainstorm a list of effects. Your teacher will write them in list form on the board. Copy the list here.**

_____ _____

_____ _____

_____ _____

C. **After you have a complete list of effects, discuss them. Decide which should be included in the paragraph. Cross out the ones that are not strong or relevant.**

Writing

Write the first draft of a paragraph about the effects of global warming.

_____

_____

_____

_____

_____

_____

_____

Revising

Read your paragraph and look for ways to improve it. Use the Revising Checklist on page 66 to help you. After you revise your paragraph, copy the final draft on a separate piece of paper.

Writing Exercise 2

Prewriting

Discuss this information with a partner.

Drinking a moderate amount of caffeine probably won't cause you any harm. But drinking too much caffeine can have negative effects on your health. Heavy caffeine use is more than 500 to 600 mg a day (four to seven cups of coffee). Here are some of the effects of too much caffeine.

- insomnia
- nervousness, anxiety
- nausea or other gastrointestinal problems
- fast or irregular heartbeat
- muscle tremors
- headaches

Writing

Use the list to write the first draft of a paragraph about the effects of too much caffeine on the human body. Begin with a topic sentence.

_____

_____

_____

_____

_____

_____

Revising

A. **Read your paragraph and look for ways to improve it. Use the Revising Checklist on page 66 to help you.**

B. **Check for errors in grammar, spelling, and punctuation. After you revise your paragraph, copy the final draft on a separate piece of paper.**

Writing Exercise 3

Prewriting

A. **Choose a topic and list the effects of that decision on your life.**

- getting married
- picking a school
- choosing a career
- buying a house
- coming to an English-speaking country

____ _____

____ _____

____ _____

____ _____

____ _____

B. **Look over your list. Cross out the ideas that are not effects of the decision. Number the effects in order of importance.**

Writing

Write the first draft of your paragraph, using your list as a guide. Remember to begin with a topic sentence.

_____

_____

_____

_____

_____

_____

_____

_____

Revising

A. Exchange paragraphs with a classmate. Give each other suggestions for improving your paragraphs. You can use the Revising Checklist on page 66 to help you.

B. Check for errors in grammar, spelling, and punctuation. Copy your revised paragraph on a separate piece of paper.

Writing Exercise 4

Prewriting

A. Read the information.

> Acton is a small town in the Midwest. It has a population of 2,500. It is a safe, quiet, and clean place to live. Most of the people have lived there all their lives and know each other very well. The town has not changed very much in the past 100 years.
>
> Last month, Stanley Manufacturing decided to open a large factory in Acton. This will bring many new people to the community. Some people are worried about the negative effects the new factory will have on the town. Other people are excited about the positive effects the new factory will have.

B. In small groups make predictions about the impact the new factory will have on Acton. Make a list of all the possible effects you can think of.

Positive Effects	Negative Effects
more jobs	pollution

Writing

Choose one of the following groups.

1. You are part of a group of conservative residents that doesn't want Acton to change. On a separate piece of paper, write a paragraph predicting the negative effects the factory will have on the town.

2. You are a member of a group of progressive residents that is open to changes in your community. On a separate piece of paper, write a paragraph predicting the positive effects the new factory will have on the town.

Revising

A. **Read over your group's paragraph and look for ways to improve it. Use the Revising Checklist on page 66 to help you.**

B. **Check for errors in grammar, spelling, and punctuation. Copy your revised paragraph on a separate piece of paper.**

Writing Exercise 5

Prewriting

A. **Work with a partner. Look at the diagram. It shows how plants and animals depend on each other in a farm pond. Discuss the diagram with your partner. Imagine that you have been asked to write a short explanation of this diagram for a children's science magazine.**

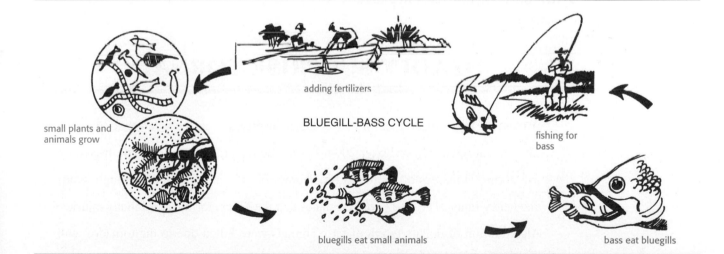

adding fertilizers

BLUEGILL-BASS CYCLE

small plants and animals grow

fishing for bass

bluegills eat small animals

bass eat bluegills

B. **Make a list of the effects that plants and animals in the pond have on each other.**

_____   _____

_____   _____

_____   _____

Writing

Write the first draft of a paragraph about the ecological relationships that are shown in the diagram on page 181. Begin with a topic sentence.

_____

_____

_____

_____

_____

_____

_____

Revising

Read your paragraph with your partner and look for ways to improve it. Use the Revising Checklist on page 66 to help you. After you revise your paragraph, copy the final draft on a separate piece of paper.

YOU BE THE EDITOR

Read the article. It contains seven mistakes. Correct the mistakes. Copy the corrected article on a separate piece of paper.

DEADLY SURPRISE TORNADO

August 3. The tornado that hit kansas today surprised even the weather forecasters. The violent winds blowed over 200 miles per hour. Much crops were destroyed by the storm. Hundreds of people lost his homes or offices because of the high winds and heavy rains. The Red Cross estimates that the killer storm caused many injuries. Also, million of dollars worth of farm animals were killed due to the tornado. will take the people of Kansas many time to recover from the effects of this tornado.

ON YOUR OWN

Choose one of these topics and write a paragraph.
- causes or effects of immigrating to a new country
- causes or effects of an unhealthy habit (smoking, overeating, drinking too much)
- causes or effects of a recent economic or political situation in your country or a country you know well

CHAPTER 13

WRITING PERSONAL LETTERS AND BUSINESS LETTERS

In this chapter you will learn how to write two kinds of letters—personal letters and business letters.

PERSONAL LETTERS

Personal letters are often called "friendly letters." They are letters that you write to a friend or relative. Personal letters include information about yourself, and ask questions about how your friend or relative is doing. Personal letters are informal and are often handwritten. There are five main parts to a personal letter.

September 8, 2010   ] DATE

Dear Daniel,   ] GREETING

    Thanks so much for the wonderful week I spent with you and your family. Your mother is such a terrific cook! I think I must have gained 10 pounds in just the seven days I spent with you. It was really nice of you to take the week off to spend time with me and show me so many places. You're lucky to live in such an exciting city. Your friends are great, and I really enjoyed meeting them. I hope you'll be able to visit my part of the country soon. Thanks again for a wonderful time. Say hi to everyone. Keep in touch.   MESSAGE

Best,   ] CLOSING

Matthew   ] SIGNATURE

Remember these guidelines when you write a personal letter.

- The date goes in the upper right corner. (The month is capitalized, and a comma goes between the date and the year.)
- The greeting ("Dear _____,") is followed by a comma.
- The closing (often "Love," in personal letters) is followed by a comma.

Use the following form for the envelope of a personal letter.

Matthew Graham
327 South 2nd Street
Philadelphia, PA 19012

RETURN ADDRESS (YOUR ADDRESS)

US

Mr. Daniel Lourie
52 Main Street
Conby, OR 99106

ADDRESSEE (PERSON RECEIVING LETTER)

Don't forget:
- Your address goes in the upper left-hand corner.
- The return address of the person who writes the letter goes in the upper left-hand corner.
- The address of the person who will receive the letter goes in the center of the envelope.
- The stamp goes in the upper right-hand corner.

Writing Personal Letters

Activity 1

Write a personal letter to a friend you haven't seen recently. Tell your friend what is new in your life. Also, ask some questions about his or her life.

_____

_____

_____

_____

_____

_____

_____

_____

_____

_____

Activity 2

A. **Write a short letter to each of the following people. Write each on a separate piece of paper. Bring to class a properly addressed envelope for each letter.**

1. Invite your **friend** to come visit you.
2. Thank your **relative** for a gift he or she sent you.
3. Tell your **parents** about an important decision you made.

B. **Exchange letters with a partner. Read your partner's letter. Pretend you are the person receiving the letter and write a response to each one.**

BUSINESS LETTERS

Business letters are more formal than personal letters. They are usually written to someone you do not know. You might write a business letter to request information or to inform someone about a problem. Look at the model business letter. There are six parts to a business letter. There are several acceptable formats you can use for a business letter, but the block format shown here is the easiest and most common. In the block format, all parts of the letter begin on the left margin.

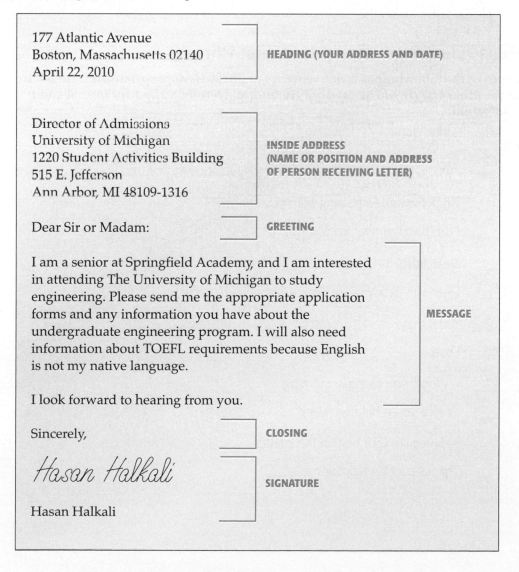

177 Atlantic Avenue
Boston, Massachusetts 02140
April 22, 2010 — **HEADING (YOUR ADDRESS AND DATE)**

Director of Admissions
University of Michigan
1220 Student Activities Building
515 E. Jefferson
Ann Arbor, MI 48109-1316 — **INSIDE ADDRESS (NAME OR POSITION AND ADDRESS OF PERSON RECEIVING LETTER)**

Dear Sir or Madam: — **GREETING**

I am a senior at Springfield Academy, and I am interested in attending The University of Michigan to study engineering. Please send me the appropriate application forms and any information you have about the undergraduate engineering program. I will also need information about TOEFL requirements because English is not my native language. — **MESSAGE**

I look forward to hearing from you.

Sincerely, — **CLOSING**

Hasan Halkali — **SIGNATURE**

Hasan Halkali

Remember these guidelines for writing business letters.

- Business letters in English almost always begins with "Dear … " even if you do not know the person. Look at the examples.

Examples:

Dear Mr. Becker:
Dear Mrs. Becker:
Dear Ms. Becker:
Dear Sir:
Dear Madam:
Dear Sir or Madam:

- Use a colon after the greeting.
- Identify yourself and state the purpose of your letter at the beginning. Go directly to the point. Be brief and clear.
- Type business letters if possible.
- Do not ask personal information (age, health, family) of the person you are writing to.
- Do not use slang, informal phrases, or contractions.
- Business letters end with a formal closing. The most common closing is "Sincerely."
- Use a comma after the closing.

Identifying Formal and Informal Phrases

In each of the following pairs, one sentence or phrase is appropriate for formal letters, but the other one should be used only in informal letters. Write *F* for formal and *I* for informal.

1. _____ I'm really sorry about what happened.

   _____ I would like to apologize for the inconvenience this caused you.

2. _____ I look forward to hearing from you soon.

   _____ I can't wait to hear from you.

3. _____ Dear Julie,

   _____ Dear Mrs. Brody:

4. _____ Yours truly,

   _____ Love,

5. _____ I will call you Monday morning.

   _____ I'll give you a call next week.

6. _____ I appreciate your help in this matter.

   _____ Thanks a lot for helping me.

Writing Exercise 1

Prewriting

Read the advertisement for the Philadelphia Orchestra.

> SEE THE
> # Philadelphia Orchestra
> Thursday, November 5 through Sunday, November 15
> ## HURRY! ORDER TICKETS NOW!
> ### Academy of Music
> 1420 Locust St., Phila., PA 19102
> EVENINGS – 8 P.M.   MATINEES – Wed, Sat, and Sun 3 P.M.
>
> | | Orchestra & Mezzanine | Balcony | | Orchestra & Mezzanine | Balcony |
> |---|---|---|---|---|---|
> | **Evenings** | | | **Matinees** | | |
> | Mon-Thurs | $30 | $25 | Wed | $25 | $20 |
> | Fri-Sat | $32 | $27 | Sat | $27 | $22 |
> | | | | Sun | $30 | $25 |

Writing

Write a letter requesting tickets. In your letter you will need to state the following:

- the date and time of the performance you want to attend
- the number and price of the tickets you want
- whether you are including your credit card number or a check

_____

_____

_____

_____

_____

_____

_____

_____

_____

_____

_____

_____

_____

Revising

A. Read your letter again. Use the Business Letter Revising Checklist and make corrections if necessary.

BUSINESS LETTER REVISING CHECKLIST	YES	NO
1. Have you included both a heading and an inside address?		
2. Is there a colon after the greeting?		
3. Is the letter direct and to the point?		
4. Is there a comma after the closing?		
5. Have you signed the letter?		
6. Is the punctuation, spelling, and grammar correct?		

B. Revise your letter and then copy it on a separate piece of paper.

Writing Exercise 2

Prewriting

Choose one of the following tasks. Make a list of ideas you want to include in your letter.
- Write to a college admissions office asking for information.
- Write to a radio station requesting more information about a product you heard advertised.
- Write a letter to a magazine publisher stating that you ordered a magazine subscription three months ago but haven't received a magazine yet.
- Write a letter of importance to you.

_____   _____

_____   _____

_____   _____

_____   _____

Writing

Write your letter on a separate piece of paper.

Revising

A. Revise your letter. Use the Business Letter Revising Checklist above to help you. Make corrections if necessary.

B. Bring your finished letter to class in a properly addressed envelope. Use the same format for a business letter envelope that you use for a personal letter envelope. Exchange letters with a classmate and give each other suggestions for improving your letters.

LETTERS OF COMPLAINT AND PRAISE

Read the following business letter and answer the questions.

1123 Gardner Street
Swansea, Massachusetts 02777
April 17, 2010

Ms. Samantha Stiller, Customer Service Manager
Beauty Glow Cosmetics Company
234 Philip Place
Oswego, New York

Dear Ms. Stiller:

   I have been using Beauty Glow products for many years, and I have always been very pleased with them. However, last week I bought a bottle of your newest perfume, Rose Petal, and I was very disappointed. First of all, the perfume stained my blouse. It also caused my skin to itch and burn. Finally, the sprayer broke the first time I used it. I feel that this product does not meet your standards of high quality. I am enclosing my receipt from the store. Please send me a refund. I look forward to hearing from you soon.

Sincerely,

Charlotte Sherden

Charlotte Sherden

1. What is Charlotte complaining about?

   _____

2. Why was she unsatisfied with the product? What three reasons does she mention?

   _____

   _____

   _____

3. What does Charlotte want the company to do?

   _____

Activity

A. **Read the situation and discuss it with a partner.**

Situation: Two weeks ago you called the person who lives above you in your apartment building. You were upset because he was playing his stereo so loudly. In fact, he often plays it very loudly all day long, so it bothers you when you are trying to study. He also plays it late at night when you are trying to sleep. When you spoke with him on the phone, he said that he would try to keep the volume lower. The first few days it was better, but now it is a problem again. You are trying to study for your final exams. It is very difficult because of the constant noise.

B. **Write a polite note to your neighbor asking him to be more considerate.**

_____

_____

_____

_____

_____

_____

_____

C. **It is now one week later and the noise has gotten even worse. You are furious. Write an angry letter to your landlord, Lorna Taylor, threatening to break your lease and move out if he or she does not do something about the noise.**

_____

_____

_____

_____

_____

_____

_____

_____

_____

_____

_____

_____

_____

_____

Writing Exercise

Prewriting

Discuss the following topics in a small group.

- a great experience you had at a hotel or restaurant
- a bad experience you had at a hotel or restaurant

Writing

Write the first draft of the body of a business letter to the manager of the hotel or restaurant. Explain the situation.

_____

_____

_____

_____

_____

_____

_____

_____

_____

_____

_____

_____

_____

Revising

A. **Exchange letters with a partner. Give each other suggestions for improving your letters. Revise your letter. You can also use the Business Letter Revising Checklist on page 188 to help you.**

B. **Copy your revised letter on a separate piece of paper.**

YOU BE THE EDITOR

Read the personal letter. It contains seven mistakes. Correct the mistakes. Copy the corrected letter on a separate piece of paper.

June 22, 2010

Dear Ben:

   I just visited the Morgan Motor Company factory in Malvern, england, and I felt like I was back in the 1920s. There are computers and other modern equipment, but I soon realized that most things have not changed. Morgans is still made the old-fashioned way. Each ones is build by hand, so no two are exactly alike, and only about ten cars are made per week. That's why there is a five-year waiting list for a new one. Morgans don't have power steering, a power brakes, or radios. But, they do have a loyals fan club. Morgan lovers can talk for hours about the thrill of feeling every bump in the road, of listening to the roar of the wind, and of smelling the sweet perfume of burning oil as you drive along. I'm enclosing a picture I took of one of the Morgans. I put my name at the waiting list for a new Morgan!

Love,

Jackson

ON YOUR OWN

Write a letter to a friend or relative. Exchange it with a classmate and give each other suggestions for improving your letters. Then address an envelope and mail the letter.

WRITING SUMMARIES

Summaries require a special kind of writing. A good summary gives only main ideas. It does not include details. Before you begin to write a summary, you need to read the article several times to make sure you understand it completely.

DISTINGUISHING BETWEEN MAIN IDEAS AND DETAILS

A. **Read the article twice. Underline the main ideas during the second reading.**

Dog Hero Is Honored

This dog hero was only nine months old when he performed his brave act. Bo, a Golden retriever, won the annual hero award from the Ken-L Ration dog food company. His prize included a gold medal, a gold collar and leash, and a year's supply of dog food! He also won $5,000 for his owners.

Bo did his brave deed last June. Bo and his owners, Rob and Laurie Roberts, were going down the Colorado River rapids in a 16-foot boat. The Roberts family lives near the river in Glenwood Springs, Colorado. Both of the Robertses, and Bo, are good swimmers. The Robertses also love boating. The June trip was Bo's first time in a boat.

Things were fine until, as Laurie Roberts said, "A 6-foot wave broke in front of us and filled the boat with water. Another big wave caught us from the back and flipped the boat over." Rob was thrown clear, but Laurie and Bo were trapped under it. "Every time I tried to escape, my head hit the boat," Laurie said. "I hit the bottom of the river several times. I realized I was drowning."

Rob picks up the story. "I reached the shore and looked for Laurie," he said. "I saw Bo swim out from under the over-turned boat. Then he turned around and dived. Soon he came back up, pulling Laurie by the hair." Laurie, scared and breathless, tried to grab Bo. But the dog stayed out of reach as if knowing they would both drown if Laurie pulled him under. Finally Laurie grabbed Bo's tail. He dragged her 30 yards to shore. Laurie was cut and bleeding, but she wasn't badly hurt.

"If it hadn't been for Bo, I wouldn't be here," Laurie told the audience at the Dog Hero awards dinner.

Ken-L Ration has been giving Dog Hero awards for twenty-nine years. In that time, hero dogs have been honored for saving the lives of 306 people.

B. Read the statements about the story "Dog Hero Is Honored." Write *MI* next to sentences that are main ideas. Write *D* next to sentences that give details.

_____ 1. Bo's prizes included a gold medal, a gold collar and leash, and a year's supply of dog food.

_____ 2. Bo won the annual hero award from the Ken-L Ration dog food company.

_____ 3. Rob and Laurie Roberts are good swimmers.

_____ 4. Bo saved Laurie's life when he rescued her from a boating accident.

_____ 5. Bo dragged Laurie 30 yards.

_____ 6. Ken-L Ration has given Dog Hero awards for 29 years.

_____ 7. Bo's brave deed happened last June.

_____ 8. Bo and his owners were going down the Colorado River rapids in a 16-foot boat.

_____ 9. Hero dogs have been honored for saving the lives of 306 people.

C. Complete the following summary.

Rob and Laurie Roberts's dog, _____, (who) won the annual

Ken-L Ration _____ (what) _____ (when)

for saving _____. (why) Rob, Laurie, and Bo were on the

_____ (where) when their boat was hit by a big wave.

The boat turned over and Laurie was trapped underneath. Bo rescued Laurie

and dragged her to _____. (where)

HOW TO WRITE A ONE-PARAGRAPH SUMMARY

The hardest part of writing a summary is deciding what to include and what to leave out. It will help if you think about the questions *Who?, When?, Where?, Why?, What?,* and *How?* Remember not to include any of your own opinions or ideas. Follow these steps:

1. Read the article once for the main idea.
2. Reread the article and underline the main points.
3. Write the first draft of your summary. Include the following:
   • a topic sentence that states the name and author of the article and the main idea
   • supporting sentences that explain, in your own words, the main points in the article
   • a final statement that summarizes any conclusions the author made in the article

Writing Exercise 1

Prewriting

A. **Read the following section from an ecology textbook.**

Why Do Some Animals Die Out?

It is natural for species of animals to become extinct over millions of years. But, over the past 200 years, humans have caused the process to speed up. In recent years, the total number of threatened animal species has increased from 5,205 to 5,435. Today 25 percent (one in four) of mammal species and 12 percent (one in eight) of bird species are threatened with extinction. In most cases this is a result of human activity. How are people accelerating the process of animal extinction?

First of all, people threaten the survival of animal species by destroying their habitats. As human populations grow, people keep building houses and factories in fields and woods. As they spread over the land, they destroy animals' homes. If the animals can't find a place to live, they die out. Sixteen kinds of Hawaiian birds have become extinct for this reason. Other animals, such as the Florida Key deer, may soon die out because they are losing their homes.

Overhunting is another way that humans are causing some animals to become extinct. In some parts of the world, the parts of rare animals are worth a lot of money. For example, some people will pay more than $1,000 for a single rhino horn. This encourages hunters to kill rhinos even though the animal faces extinction. Other animals that are threatened with extinction from overhunting include the blue whale, the mountain gorilla, and the cheetah.

Humans are also polluting the air, water, and soil. The effect of pollution on animal species can be complicated. For example, when waste from factories is dumped into rivers, the rivers become polluted. The fish that live in the river are poisoned and many of them die. In addition, birds that eat the poisoned fish become poisoned themselves. Once they are poisoned, these birds cannot lay strong, healthy eggs. Fewer and fewer new birds are born. So far, no animals have become extinct because of pollution. But some, such as the brown pelican, have become rare and may die out.

Finally, when humans introduce new species into certain environments, the animals that already live there become threatened and face extinction. For example, when European settlers brought rabbits and foxes to Australia, they killed off many native Australian animals, including the bandicoot. The rabbits and foxes adapted to the Australian environment very quickly and multiplied rapidly. Eventually, the foxes hunted and killed many bandicoots for food. The rabbits took over the bandicoot habitats. Now the bandicoots are threatened with extinction in their own land.

B. **Now answer the following questions.**

1. What is the section about?

   _____

2. Why is it happening?

   _____

3. Who is responsible?

   _____

4. When is it happening?

   _____

Writing

Write a one-paragraph summary of the section. State the main idea of the section in the first sentence. Answer the questions *What?*, *When?*, and *How?* in the rest of the paragraph.

_____

_____

_____

_____

_____

_____

_____

_____

_____

Revising

A. **Does your paragraph answer all of the questions in Exercise B? Look at the Revising Checklist on page 66. Exchange papers with a partner and edit each other's papers. Did you both include the same information? If not, what are the differences?**

B. **Check for errors in grammar, spelling, and punctuation. Copy your revised summary on a separate piece of paper.**

Writing Exercise 2

Prewriting

A. Read the article twice. Underline the main ideas during the second reading.

HURRICANE STRIKES—MANY HURT

Hurricane Irene hit southeastern Florida on Friday night, causing damage and destruction everywhere. The storm dumped 18 inches of rain on the area. The high winds that blew up to 85 miles per hour were responsible for most of the damage to the area. The winds knocked down trees and power lines, broke hotel windows, and damaged roofs. The wind also was to blame for ten serious injuries and several car accidents.

Much of the city was without electricity and water this morning. In fact, hundreds of thousands of people have no electricity.

The hurricane caused severe flooding. Hundreds of people lost their homes or offices because of high winds and heavy rains. Some of the worst flooding was in Miami, where police sometimes needed boats to get through up to 4 feet of standing water.

Thousands of acres of crops were damaged or destroyed in South Florida, which supplies 75 percent of the nation's winter produce. No one knows yet exactly how much money was lost in crop damage. "I could not give you an estimate of damage to the crops, but I would not be surprised if it were $100 million," said the mayor of Miami.

Local officials called Irene the worst storm of the hurricane season for the area. It will take the people of Florida a long time to recover from the effects of this hurricane.

B. Make a list of the important facts in the article. Try to include *Who?*, *What?*, *When?*, *Where?*, *Why?*, and *How?* on your list.

_____

_____

_____

_____

_____

_____

_____

C. Study your list. Make sure you have included only the main ideas. Cross out any details.

Writing

Write a short, one-paragraph summary of the article.

_____

_____

_____

_____

_____

_____

Revising

Compare your summary with some of your classmates' summaries. Have you included too much information? Did you miss an important idea? Did you include any of your own ideas? Revise your summary and then copy the final draft on a separate piece of paper.

Activity

A. **Read the following story. Discuss it with your classmates.**

The Sweetest Melody
(A Folk Tale from Afghanistan)

Long ago, there lived a shah (king) of Persia named Abbas who was clever and wise. He was curious about the world and often asked riddles. One day the shah was talking to four of his advisers, discussing music and art and life. Suddenly the shah asked, "What is the sweetest melody?"

The first adviser immediately answered, "Without question, the melody of the flute is the sweetest. It sounds like a bird singing in a tree." The second adviser spoke up. "No, no, you have it all wrong. The melody of the harp is by far the sweetest. It sounds as beautiful as the music that is played in heaven." Then the third adviser said, "You are both wrong. In all of the universe, the melody of the violin has the most pleasing sound. It can play loudly and boldly. It can play softly and sweetly. When a man hears it, he feels like someone is strumming his own heart."

The first three advisers argued bitterly. But the fourth adviser, Zaki, just watched quietly. Finally, the other three advisers looked at Shah Abbas to find out which of them was right. But the shah was looking at Zaki, who was the wisest of them all. But still he said nothing. He just sat there listening without offering his opinion. Then, the shah sent them all from the room.

Several days passed. Then, Zaki invited Shah Abbas and the other advisers to a banquet in their honor. That evening, the best and most renowned musicians in the land played all kinds of instruments, including the flute, harp, and violin. The music was exquisite, but there was no food on the table. "How strange," the advisers noticed. "There is a table here but no food." Usually at these banquets, the tables would be filled with all kinds of food. Even after guests had finished eating, the waiters would keep bringing out more and more food.

But this night was different. Although the music was plentiful, the table was empty. Where was the food? The guests' stomachs began to rumble with hunger. They looked around hopefully for the great dishes of meat and rice they expected. "We've been here for hours!" they thought to themselves. "We will starve." It was nearly midnight. And still they waited. Finally, Zaki called for the waiter. The waiter brought an enormous pot of hot food into the room. Zaki lifted the metal lid off the pot and hit it with a silver spoon. "Clung! Clung!" The sound rang through the silent room like a great bell.

All the guests smiled in relief. The wise adviser smiled at the shah and said, "The sound of food to a hungry man—that is the sweetest melody!" Suddenly, the shah spoke up in excitement. "Yes," he said to Zaki. "That is the answer."

B. **Complete the summary of "The Sweetest Melody."**

"The Sweetest Melody" is a story about _____

_____ .

One day the shah asked _____, "What is _____?"

Three of the advisers gave different answers. The first answered _____

_____ .

The second said _____ ,

and the third said _____ .

They argued, but Zaki, the fourth and wisest adviser, didn't answer.

_____ , Zaki invited the shah and his advisers to a banquet.

There were many musicians, but there was no food on the table. As the

night continued, the guests got _____ . _____ ,

a waiter brought in a big pot of food. Zaki hit the lid of the pot with

a large spoon. Then he smiled and said, "The sound of food to a

hungry man—_____ !"

Writing Exercise 3

Prewriting

A. **Read the story and discuss it with a partner.**

The Great Minu

Long ago, there was a poor man from a small town in the hills of Africa. His name was Younde. He was a simple farmer who had never been far from home. One day he had to travel from his own little village to Accra, a big city near the ocean. He had heard about Accra and all the wonderful things there, but he had never seen it. He walked for many days. The road was hot and dusty. When he came close to Accra, he saw a little boy with a great herd of cows. He wondered who owned them. Younde asked the little boy, "Who is the owner of all these cows?" But the boy didn't understand Younde. Why? Younde's language was Akim, but the boy spoke Ga, the language of Accra. Finally the little boy said "Minu," which means "I don't understand" in the Ga language. But Younde thought that "Minu" was the name of the owner of the cows, so he exclaimed, "Mr. Minu must be very rich to own so many cows."

Then Younde entered the town. He saw women selling beautiful and extravagant things at the market. "Where do all these things come from?" he asked a woman. She smiled and said, "Minu." Younde was surprised. Again he said, "Mr. Minu must be very rich to own so many beautiful things."

After that, Younde saw a fine large building surrounded by beautiful gardens. Of course, he wondered who owned it. But once again, the man he asked could not understand Younde's question, so he also answered, "Minu." Younde couldn't believe his ears. "What a rich man Mr. Minu must be! He lives in such a huge and beautiful house!" cried Younde.

Next, Younde came to the beach. There he saw many fishing boats. Younde asked a fisherman, "Who owns all these boats?" "Minu," replied the fisherman. Again Younde misunderstood the answer. "These boats belong to the Great Minu aiso! He is the richest man I have ever heard of!" cried Younde. He was very impressed with everything he saw in Accra.

Finally, Younde started to walk home. As he passed down one of the streets of the town he saw a funeral procession. Several men were carrying a coffin. Many people, all dressed in black, were walking behind the coffin. Younde asked one of the mourners[1] the name of the dead person. The mourner sadly replied, "Minu." "Poor Mr. Minu!" cried Younde. "The Great Minu is dead. He has died just like an ordinary person!"

"Poor Minu!" he said over and over again. Younde continued on his way out of the city, but he couldn't get the tragedy of Minu from his mind. "Poor Minu! So he has had to leave all his wealth and beautiful things and die just as a poor person would do! Well, well—in the future I will be content with my small house and little money." And Younde went home quite pleased, back to his own little town.

[1] **mourners:** *people who attend a funeral*

B. Make a list of the important facts in the story. Try to include *Who?*, *What?*, *When?*, *Where?*, *Why?*, and *How?* on your list.

_____

_____

_____

_____

C. Study your list. Make sure you have included only the main ideas. Cross out any details.

Writing

Write a one-paragraph summary of the story.

_____

_____

_____

_____

_____

_____

_____

_____

Revising

A. Compare your summary with some of your classmates' summaries. As you are revising, think about these questions.

1. Did you include too much information?
2. Did you miss an important idea?
3. Did you use time order to organize the sentences in your summary?

B. Check for errors in grammar, spelling, and punctuation. Copy your revised summary on a separate piece of paper.

ON YOUR OWN

Find an article on the Internet or in a book, magazine, or newspaper. Read it carefully and write a one-paragraph summary of it. Bring the article and your summary to class. Exchange summaries with a classmate and give each other suggestions for improving the summary.

ANSWERING TEST QUESTIONS

Teachers and professors often ask you to answer questions in paragraph form on tests or assignments. There are several important things to remember when answering test questions.

- Read the entire question carefully. Underline key words in the question.
- Make sure you understand exactly what information you are being asked to write about (reasons, definitions, similarities, etc.).
- Plan your answer.
- Budget your time.

One way to begin your answer is to change the question into a statement and use this statement as your topic sentence. (Sometimes the "question" is not written in question form, but in the imperative form.) Study the example.

Example:

Question: Why are giant pandas in the wild threatened with extinction?

Topic sentence: There are several reasons why giant pandas in the wild are threatened with extinction.

Activity 1

Change the following test questions into topic sentences.

1. Question: Why is unemployment rising?

   _____

   _____

2. Question: What are the effects of radiation on the human body?

   _____

   _____

3. Question: Explain the reasons ice hockey is a dangerous sport.

   _____

   _____

4. Question: Explain the importance of Abraham Lincoln in American history.

   _____

   _____

5. Question: What were the causes of the Great Depression?

   _____

   _____

6. Question: How can genetically modified plants help solve the food shortage problem?

_____

_____

7. Question: What are the advantages and disadvantages of solar energy?

_____

_____

8. Question: Describe the four kinds of clouds.

_____

_____

9. Question: Describe the four stages involved in cell division.

_____

_____

Activity 2

Read the test question and student answer. Then discuss the questions in groups.

Question: Describe the three branches of government in the United States.

> The United States' government has three main branches. The first branch is the legislative branch, which is called the Congress. Congress makes our laws. It is divided into two parts: the Senate and House of Representatives. The Senate has 100 members, two from each state, who are elected for 6-year terms. The House of Representatives is made up of 435 members who are elected for 2-year terms. The number of representatives each state has is determined by its population. The second branch is the executive branch. The job of this branch is to ensure that the laws of the United States are obeyed. The President of the United States is the head of the executive branch. The president also directs national defense and foreign policy. This branch is very big and includes the Vice President, department heads (Cabinet members), and heads of other agencies. Finally, the third branch is called the judicial branch, which is headed by the Supreme Court. It oversees the court system of the United States. Its powers include interpreting the Constitution, and reviewing laws. It also settles disagreements between individuals and the government.

1. Does the topic sentence restate the question?

_____

2. Does the answer describe each branch of government?

_____

3. Underline the signal words the student used.

4. What specific information (details such as numbers and times) did the student include?

_____

_____

_____

WRITING RESPONSES TO TEST QUESTIONS

Use the information in the boxes to answer the following test question.

Question: Discuss the similarities between the eye and the camera.

The Eye

The human eye has an iris that gets bigger or smaller to let in the right amount of light. It also has a lens that focuses the light into a clear picture. In the eye, light forms a picture on the retina. The nerve cells in the retina send a picture message to the brain. The picture the brain receives is upside down. The brain then interprets the message so that what you see is right side up.

The Camera

The camera has a diaphragm that gets bigger or smaller to let in the right amount of light. It also has a lens that focuses the light into a clear picture. In a camera, light forms a picture on film. The picture is upside down on the film.

_____

_____

_____

_____

_____

_____

_____

_____

_____

_____

_____

YOU BE THE EDITOR

Read the answer a student wrote. It contains ten mistakes. Correct the mistakes. Copy the answer on a separate piece of paper.

Question: How do languages change?

Languages change and evolve over time, much in the same way as cultures change. One way languages changes is by adding new words. This often happens through contact and interaction with another languages, often through travel and trade. This results in the borrowing of words. For example, when people from different places trade with each others, they picked up specifics words and phrases for trade objects. languages also change as they develop news words for new technologies and ideas. For instance, the words *biometrics*, *crunk*, *ginormous*, and *Sudoku* has all been added to official english dictionaries in the past a few years.

YOU BE THE EDITOR ANSWER KEY

Chapter 1, p. 9

Many of the stories in my country, ~~turkey~~ [Turkey], are about a clever man named ~~nasreddin~~ [Nasreddin]. In one story, ~~nasreddin~~ [Nasreddin] is walking through the marketplace when an angry shopkeeper stops him. The shopkeeper yells at ~~nasreddin~~ [Nasreddin] for not paying the seventy-five piasters he owes him. But the clever Nasreddin says, "~~you~~ [You] know that ~~i~~ [I] plan to pay you thirty-five piasters tomorrow, and next ~~tuesday~~ [Tuesday] another thirty-five. ~~that~~ [That] means ~~i~~ [I] owe you only five piasters. You should be ashamed for yelling at me so loudly for a debt of only five piasters!" I laugh every time I think of that story.

Chapter 2, p. 28

Erik ~~enjoy~~ [enjoys] many types of sports. He ~~is liking~~ [likes] team sports such as basketball, soccer, and baseball. In fact, he is the ~~Captain~~ [captain] of the basketball team at our school. ~~erik~~ [Erik] also plays individual sports like squash, tennis, and golf very ~~good~~ [well]. Last year he ~~win~~ [won] two golf tournaments and most of the tennis matches he played. His ~~favorites~~ [favorite] sports involve ~~dangerous~~ [danger] as well as excitement. He is ~~no~~ [not] afraid to go extreme skiing or skydiving. It was not a surprise when Erik won the sports award at graduation this year.

Chapter 3, p. 40

Throughout history, people have done mathematical computations and
kept accounts. ~~in~~ *In* early times, people used groups of sticks or stones to help
make calculations. Then the abacus was developed in ~~china. This~~ *China. These* simple
methods represent the beginnings of data processing? As computational needs
became more complicated, people developed more advanced technologies.
In 1642, Blaise ~~pascal~~ *Pascal* developed the first simple adding machine in ~~france.~~ *France.*
Later, in England in 1830, ~~charles~~ *Charles* Babbage designed the first machine that did
calculations and ~~printing~~ *printed* out results. Finally, ~~In~~ *in* the middle of the twentieth
century, researchers at the University of ~~pennsylvania builded~~ *Pennsylvania built* the first
electronic computer. Today, of course, we have the computer to perform all
kinds of advanced $_x$mathematical computations.

Chapter 4, p. 51

Corn is one of the most important food sources ~~on~~ *in* the world, but it ~~have~~ *has*
many ~~another~~ *other* important uses as well. One of the most ~~valuables~~ *valuable* uses of corn
is as an alternative energy source. Ethanol, which is ~~make~~ *made* from corn, is used
to fuel cars and planes. ~~some~~ *Some* houses are even heated with ethanol fuel. Corn
is also used to make plastics and fabrics. In fact, corn ~~are~~ *is* used in thousands of
products such as glue, shoe polish, aspirin, ink, and cosmetics. The syrup from
corn sweetens ~~Ice~~ *ice* cream, soda, and candy. Scientists continue to ~~researches~~ *research*
new uses of corn and find more every year.

Chapter 5, p. 60

The ~~triangle~~ *triangular* continent of ~~south america~~ *South America* is quite large. It stretches from

north of the equator down nearly to the Antarctic Circle. South America

has three ~~differents~~ *different* kinds of landscapes. ~~in~~ *In* the west, the magnificent ~~andes~~ *Andes*

Mountains rise all along the whole ~~pacific ocean~~ *Pacific Ocean* coast. They extend along

the entire continent from ~~northern~~ *north* to south. There are rainforests in the

Amazon ~~valley~~ *Valley* and along the Caribbean coast that cover most of the north and

northeast. In the south are the grasslands and pampas that go down to the

rocky point at the bottom of the continent called Cape Horn.

Chapter 6, p. 72

There are several ~~thing~~ *things* you can do to enhance your performance on an

exam. First, ~~Make~~ *make* sure to get a good night's sleep the night before the test.

~~that~~ *That* means sleeping for at least eight ~~hour~~ *hours*. It is also important to eat a good

breakfast the morning of the exam, so ~~You~~ *you* won't ~~have~~ *be* hungry during the exam.

Finally, bring a bottle of water to the test in case you ~~got~~ *get* thirsty. Just don't

drink too much, or you may have to get up in the middle of the exam for a

bathroom break.

Chapter 7, p. 95

Skyscrapers are on the rise. A new building called Burj Dubai in the United

Arab Emirates city of ~~dubai~~ *Dubai* is being built and will be about 2,684 ~~feets~~ *feet* tall. That

will make it the ~~taller~~ *tallest* building in the world. Until recently, the world's tallest

building was in Taipei, Taiwan. ~~this~~ *This* towering office building in the heart of the

busy capital city boasts 101 floors, which is where it gets ~~it's~~ *its* name, Taipei 101.

Recently, however, engineers and architects in Saudi Arabia announced plans

to build a skyscraper that will surpass both Taipei 101 and Burj Dubai in ~~high~~ *height*.

The Mile-High Tower, as it is being called, will be twice as tall as the Burj Dubai.

With so many tall buildings all over the world, tourists will have to get ~~use~~ *used* to

looking up more often.

Chapter 8, p. 107

It is not difficult to remove the shell from a lobster if you follow these

~~step~~ *steps*. First, you should ~~to~~ put the lobster on ~~it's~~ *its* back and remove the two large

claws and tail section. After that, ~~You~~ *you* must also twist off the flippers at *the* end of *the*

tail section. After these are twisted off, use ~~you~~ *your* fingers to push the lobster meat

out of the tail in one piece. Next, remove the black vein ~~From~~ *from* the tail meat.

Finally, before you sit down to enjoy your meal, break open the claws with a

nutcracker and remove the meat.

Chapter 9, p. 126

Dog Missing

My adorable dog, Bette, is missing. She is a small black poodle with
~~browns~~ *brown* eyes. ~~her~~ *Her* hair is short and curly. Bette weighs 8 pounds and is about
one and a half ~~foots~~ *feet* long. She has a short tail, long, floppy ears, and small
feet. She is ~~wear~~ *wearing* a silver collar with an ID tag on it. She is very friendly around
people and ~~love~~ *loves* children. I have had Bette for six years, since she was a puppy.
I ~~missing~~ *miss* her very much. I am offering a $50 reward for anyone ~~which~~ *who* finds
Bette. Please call me at 305-892-7671.

Chapter 10, p. 141

In my opinion, Suleiman was one of the greatest leaders of all time. He
accomplished more than any ~~others~~ *other* ruler of the Ottoman Empire. During his
reign ~~at~~ *from* 1520 to 1566, Suleiman ~~expanding~~ *expanded* the size of the Ottoman Empire
to include parts of Asia, ~~europe~~ *Europe*, and Africa. While ~~Suleimans~~ *Suleiman's* military ~~victorys~~ *victories*
made him a well-respected world leader, he did many ~~another~~ *other* important
things for the empire as well. For example, Suleiman introduced a new system
of laws. He also promoted ~~educate~~ *education*, architecture, and the arts. Therefore, I
~~belief~~ *believe* he deserves the name "Suleiman the Magnificent."

| Send | Reply | Forward | Move | Print | Delete | ▲ ▼ |

Subject: Madrid and Barcelona

From:

To: myfriend@institute.edu

Hi,

This is just a short message to let you know that we are back from ~~my~~ *our* trip to Spain. ~~It~~ *^* was a great vacation. Here is a picture of us outside our hotel. We went to ~~madrid~~ *Madrid* and Barcelona. Both ~~is~~ *are* great cities, and I was ~~surprise~~ *surprised* at the differences between them. First of all, the cultures are different and the people speak ~~differents~~ *different* dialects. Madrid is also ~~more~~ bigger and ~~busiest~~ *busier* than Barcelona. Madrid is more crowded ~~to~~ *than* Barcelona. Luckily, the weather was sunny, warm, and beautiful in Barcelona, but it rained the whole time we were in Madrid!

Now that I am back, let's set a date for the next committee meeting.

Jane

DEADLY SURPRISE TORNADO

August 3. The tornado that hit ~~kansas~~ *Kansas* today surprised even the weather forecasters. The violent winds ~~blowed~~ *blew* over 200 miles per hour. ~~Much~~ *Many* crops were destroyed by the storm. Hundreds of people lost ~~his~~ *their* homes or offices because of the high winds and heavy rains. The Red Cross estimates that the killer storm caused many injuries. Also, ~~million~~ *millions* of dollars worth of farm animals were killed due to the tornado. *It* ~~will~~ take the people of Kansas ~~many~~ *a lot of* time to recover from the effects of this tornado.

June 22, 2010

Dear Ben,

    I just visited the Morgan Motor Company factory in Malvern, ~~england~~, *England*

and I felt like I was back in the 1920s. There are computers and other modern

equipment, but I soon realized that most things have not changed. Morgans

~~is~~ *are* still made the old-fashioned way. Each ~~ones~~ *one* is ~~build~~ *built* by hand, so no two

are exactly alike, and only about ten cars are made per week. That's why there

is a five-year waiting list for a new one. Morgans don't have power steering,

~~a~~ power brakes, or radios. But, they do have a ~~loyals~~ *loyal* fan club. Morgan lovers

can talk for hours about the thrill of feeling every bump in the road, of listening

to the roar of the wind, and of smelling the sweet perfume of burning oil as

you drive along. I'm enclosing a picture I took of one of the Morgans. I put my

name ~~at~~ *on* the waiting list for a new Morgan!

Love,

Jackson

Languages change and evolve over time, much in the same way as

cultures change. One way languages ~~changes~~ [change] is by adding new words. This

often happens through contact and interaction with ~~another~~ [other] languages, often

through travel and trade. This results in the borrowing of words. For example,

when people from different places trade with each ~~others~~ [other], they ~~picked~~ [pick] up

~~specifics~~ [specific] words and phrases for trade objects. ~~languages~~ [Languages] also change as they

develop ~~news~~ [new] words for new technologies and ideas. For instance, the words

biometrics, *crunk*, *ginormous*, and *Sudoku* ~~has~~ [have] all been added to official

~~english~~ [English] dictionaries in the past ~~a~~ few years.